Confessions
of a Session Singer

Scandalous Secrets of Success Behind the Mic

Get Inside the Head of
One of the Music Industry's
Most Successful Session Singers

by Mak Kaylor

Backbeat
Books

BACKBEAT BOOKS

AN IMPRINT OF HAL LEONARD CORPORATION

NEW YORK

Published in 2007 by
Backbeat Books (an imprint of Hal Leonard Corporation)
19 West 21st Street, New York, NY 10010

Printed in the United States of America

Book design by Mark Lerner

Library of Congress Cataloging-in-Publication Data is available upon request.
ISBN-10: 0-87930-911-3
ISBN-13: 978-0-87930-911-4

www.backbeatbooks.com

*My "confessions" are dedicated to the
gifted songwriters who have paid
for the hard-earned lessons
I have learned in the recording studio.*

Contents

Acknowledgments

Thank you to Richard Johnston, for keeping your word; to Backbeat Books and the Hal Leonard staff, for keeping the fire burning; and to Bob Doerschuk, for your brilliance. Thank you to my girls—LeAnn and Macy—for understanding and supporting my calling to write. And thank you, God, for the music of life.

Introduction

I began this love affair with her at a very young age. I've spent more nights in dim lit rooms than I can even count . . . caught up in her spell. I've fulfilled my wildest fantasies with her in the middle of the day and in the wee hours. Time flies when we're together. I forget the world out there beyond the walls and windows that contain the magic we're creating. I tell my family and friends that I'll see them soon—but they've learned that it will be much later. She holds me captive and I don't want to leave her. I reveal my deepest emotions to her. . . . I experience something new and exciting every time I'm with her . . . yet . . . I feel at home with her. . . . She is my mistress. . . . She is . . . the recording studio.

All of this *film noir* verbiage is merely in fun, but the truth is that you *do* need to have a passion for singing professionally in the studio if you plan to start and maintain a career as a session singer. A love affair *does* exist between a session singer and the recording studio. It's been over 25 years since I first darkened the doors of a studio, and I still get a thrill from slipping the headphones on and *laying down* (recording) a vocal, from getting the headphone mix just the way I like it, with a perfect *track-to-vocal ratio* (volume balance of band and my vocal), from the exact amount of *wetness* (reverb) to making sure the *talkback* is *hot* enough (making sure the engineer's communication with me through the headphones is at a good audible level) in my *cans* (headphones) coming from the engineer at the *console* (mixing board in the control room.)

I'm sure that other session pros would agree that stepping up to the *mic* (microphone) is like a pro ballplayer knocking the dirt off his cleats and stepping up to the plate, the pilot preparing for take-off and lifting off the tarmac or the architect sitting down at the drafting table with a fresh set of plans. Even after years of experience as a session singer working primarily in Nashville, the desire for excellence is still what drives me to saddle up and render another song!

It's been my privilege to work with some of the most successful songwriters, music publishers, and producers in the music industry. The information and stories gleaned from years behind the mic provide the background for this book. Through leading music industry seminars and workshops, giving music career lectures to industry hopefuls, or simply counseling individual students, I'm able to tailor *Confessions* to the needs of anyone interested in a professional studio career. Songwriters, audio engineers, and producers will benefit from getting inside the head of a studio vocalist, by learning what to expect from their hired gun and what's expected of them in the recording process. This information will also help studio musicians who want to rejuvenate their careers. You may simply want to know more about this unique trade while enjoying a few anecdotes acquired from my years as a session singer, or you may seriously need to know more about the recording process to improve your work. Either way, I'm glad to have you in the *cage* (vocal booth) with me.

So, what *is* the secret to success in this business? C'mon, do you really think I'm going to answer that question in the Introduction? Success is subjective anyway. Your definition of success may differ from mine. Making a living as a singer may be your goal—or maybe doing session work is a means to another end. In Nashville, recording artists such as Alan Jackson, Garth Brooks, Trisha Yearwood, and Linda Davis all began their recording careers in the trenches as demo singers. One of the busiest demo singers in town for several years was eventual *Nashville Star* winner Buddy Jewell.

There are many avenues you can travel to reach your goal, but whichever path you choose, my true confessions of personal trials, tips, and anecdotes are yours to share in the hope that you will achieve your own version of success.

Just as there is whimsical wording in the world of Mafioso and mobsters (as my chapter titles reference in fun), professional singers and players in the studio have their own slang terminology. You'll see a lot of this lingo throughout *Confessions*, but I'll make sure to define all of it. The more familiar you are with the terms that we studio-tanned "cave dwellers" use, the more you'll fit into this sometimes glamorized, sometimes underrated, and often misunderstood vocation.

Session work can seem like a racket to those who are trying to break into the system, but despite the gangster jargon, there is nothing criminal or immoral in the information you are about to read. There is no underworld when it comes to legitimate session work although there is almost a secret club connection between professional session singers and players. We will discuss ways you can join the exclusive club—without a secret handshake or even a password!

If you view studio work as a hobby, by all means, keep it that way. If you intend to make studio sessions your life's work, or you want to just try it out for a season, you must treat it as serious business.

My confessions are just beginning. Join me as I come clean with classified information usually reserved for those of us who have spent a lifetime behind the mic.

It's time to begin, so to quote the most exciting phrase a session singer can ever hear . . . a phrase that means it's time to "shut up and sing". . . .

We're red. . . .

CHAPTER 1

Who Do You Have to Sleep With to Get This Gig?

How to Become a Professional Session Vocalist

Well, of course, the answer to the question is "nobody"—if you're legitimate. Books and television have perpetuated the notion that becoming bedfellows with key players in the entertainment industry is the first step toward success. Good business relationships are vital for success and longevity in the recording industry. These relationships are most often made in a professional manner and have more to do with building trust rather than compromise. Truth is, there's nothing risqué about that first step up on the ladder to success as a session singer. Instead, it's all about preparation.

You've taken that first step already, by reading this book. But before going much further, let's cut to the chase.

Why Do You Want to Be a Session Singer?

Think about it. It's important to know your reasons for pursuing this vocation and to have a plan before giving it your best shot.

Do you think it's a glamorous gig because you get to work with music industry professionals? Is it a means to an end or do you intend to make it your life's work? Do you simply want to be more comfortable in the recording studio so that you can apply what you learn to your own artistic endeavors? Are you only interested in the money? Do you just think it would be a *cool* gig? Are you looking for an *easy* gig?

(If your answer is yes to the last question, then you've got a lot of learning left to do. Crafting a song vocally can be fun, but it's never really easy.)

There *is* money to be made if you handle your business well. In fact, a session vocalist with regular clients—producers, songwriters, music publishers, or studio owners—can enjoy a steady income, while artists signed to record labels are in and out of deals all the time.

A few years ago, while attending an event hosted by EMI Music Publishing during Country Music Association Awards week, a fellow session singer and friend approached me about a new recording deal I had just signed with Sony Productions. "So I hear you've got a record deal, Makky." Expecting him to congratulate me, I said confidently, "Yeah, I'm pretty excited about it," to which he replied, "Why would you want to give up a steady gig as a session singer to do that?" My balloon was somewhat deflated when I realized that what he said was true. I knew a lot more recording artists without deals—even established artists—than I knew out-of-work session singers. Sure enough, he was right. Several months later, the sides (songs) we had recorded flopped because of position changes in the company.

As if to make the point even clearer, people at the label asked me to slow down on the demo work I was doing, and so when my record deal fizzled out, I had to start over with my clients to get back into the session world. Record labels often ask you to stop doing demo sessions because underhanded, desperate sharks (I call them "au-

dio paparazzi") will sometimes try to sell your demos after you've become a name artist, therefore peddling bootleg product.

Think about why you want to be a professional studio singer, then make a plan using some of the information you're about to read.

The Big Questions

At almost every workshop or seminar I lead, the questions arise: "How in the world do you become a session singer?" "Who do you have to know?" or "How can you make a living doing *that*?" is the often unspoken follow-up. Well, you don't have to be the producer's nephew or the music publisher's sister to land work as a session vocalist. It *is* possible to crack open the airtight doors of the recording industry if you're prepared and if you apply what I refer to as the Six Safecrackers:

Talent, Confidence, Courtesy—Tenacity, Courage, and Commitment—(TCC—TCC)!

Six Safecrackers for Success

(1) Talent. You'll need the *pipes*, the *goods*, the *chops*, before a producer, music publisher, or songwriter will spend part of their budget to have you work on their session. This seems obvious, but you'd be surprised at how many people move to a music mecca such as Nashville, L.A., or New York assuming they have the talent to be a professional singer only to find out the hard way that even if they're good singers, they don't have the ability to compete in the big leagues.

Let me be honest with you. Being a good club singer or church singer won't guarantee you a role in the professional world of recording—not until you develop certain nuances and skills.

Sure, you need a good deal of natural ability. But that ability must be shaped and sharpened to its maximum capacity. This is accomplished not merely in theory but through plenty of time behind the mic in the recording studio.

A vocalist cannot be trained to possess instincts. *Instincts* are natural. *Skills* are acquired. In the vocal booth, you've got to have instincts before acquiring any recording skills. Vocalists doing professional session work are often self-trained, having learned what makes for commercial success by real-world experience, rather than classically trained. Of course, a classically trained singer can possibly learn in time to sing commercially and with relevant emotion. It's just much harder to lock into a marketable groove once you've been taught *technique* rather than *communication*. (I'll expound later on the relevance of vocal communication as opposed to technique and its application to mainstream music.)

One other thing: Although classically trained vocalists often have a harder time singing with mainstream marketability, *maintenance training* such as proper care, strengthening, and endurance exercise do enhance a vocalist's God-given abilities. Hopefully, you will need to know how to keep your voice healthy and strong because of a busy session schedule!

First, though, it is imperative that you know without a doubt that you have the talent it takes to survive in the highly competitive world of recording. *Know* you're good before embarking on your career. How can you know for sure? Ask a professional, not a friend or relative, for advice and feedback. A professional will more likely give you an unbiased opinion. If the pro's response is negative but you're still convinced you have what it takes to be a successful session singer, then prove them wrong. Remember, the music industry is based on opinions!

At the beginning, you will endear yourself to potential clients if you have the humility to know that there is skill needed that a rookie off the street simply cannot possess without spending hours behind the microphone. Realize your need to learn more as you begin this trade. In fact, hunger for it!

Contradictory though it sounds, a combination of confidence and genuine humility will carry your talent a great distance. Be humble yet confident of your abilities as a vocalist.

(2) Confidence. You must exude confidence to potential clients, producers, music publishers, songwriters, and studio managers. There are lots of formidable singers. The music industry is not for the timid. But there is a difference between confidence and arrogance. That difference is what I call "the karate mentality."

I once asked a musician friend with a black belt in karate if he had ever hurt anybody who gave him trouble at a nightclub gig. He told me that just *knowing* he could break them into pieces was enough. He doesn't have to *do* anything except in competitions. He exudes confidence in conflict because he has confidence in what he can do. The same confidence applies to marketing your abilities to sing professionally. If you're sure of your vocal strengths, then there is no need to wear arrogance as a cover for your lack of ability. Be confident without arrogance or timidity as you begin to network with recording industry professionals—and use common courtesy.

(3) Courtesy. As I mentioned earlier and will mention again because of its importance, the recording industry is based on relationships. Your gifts as a singer will only take you so far. Your relationships within the industry will sustain your career. Thus, courtesy (the way you treat everyone) is essential to building lasting business relationships. In the music industry, it's quite common to know the names of colleagues' chil-

dren, their hometowns, and even their health issues. As you search for sessions, remember that you are not just trying to make a buck in the short term. You are actually forming alliances that will have positive long-term benefits. It's an investment, something like insurance.

Speaking of insurance, health issues, and lasting business relationships . . .

I had been one of the most in demand session singers on Music Row for several years, as well as a songwriter and artist, when I started feeling tired a lot. It got to the point that I often had to sit down between vocal takes. I had also noticed that I was short on air from time to time. Eventually, I was diagnosed with a serious heart defect and had to undergo open-heart surgery. (My heart was working at about 20% capacity and had tripled in size.)

You don't just jump right back into professional vocal work after having open-heart surgery, so I took a few months to recuperate. But although I had gained my vocal strength back in time, I wondered if I could still go back to the same clients for work.

In time, I did. And I was surprised that the business associates with whom I had built relationships over the years greeted me supportively, with trust rather than doubting my abilities to perform. They were really more interested in my health and financial condition than they were about how well I might perform since undergoing the surgery. (Fortunately, I was singing better than ever!) It was easier to get back in the saddle than I assumed it would be because of the good and genuine business relationships I had built through the years.

These business relationships, by the way, extend to anyone and everyone. Be as kind to the receptionist as you are to the studio owner. In the recording industry, you never know who plays an important role nor do you know what position someone may have in the future. I've known interns who have become creative directors at major publishing companies and record executives who became car salesmen because their labels went out of business. "Musical chairs" is played constantly in the music industry, so be kind to everyone you meet.

As career development director at an illustrious international audio engineering school, I take pleasure in helping young, talented students get started in the recording industry.

For example, I've been able to convince many of the top recording studios to acquire studio interns from the school. On one occasion, when I was invited to meet a studio manager, I was greeted by a young lady who, at first glance, appeared to be the receptionist. I was kind and courteous and she asked me wait a moment while she called the manager. She then said, "Hi, I'm the business manager here at the studio. I'll take you to meet the studio manager and we can talk about our needs here and how we might help one another out."

If I had been the least bit condescending, I'm sure her response would have been quite different. Instead, because I'd treated her respectfully, I had been given an open door. This same scenario has played out many times. Respect and courtesy will usually open doors for you!

When you make contact with a decision maker, don't under any circumstances talk ill of anyone else in the industry. You never know who might be listening.

I took my little girl for a burger and shake one night. Sitting at the next table was a rather large and loudmouthed "gentleman" who had obviously brought a first date. He was bragging about his role in the music industry and all of the key players that he knows. My guess is that he most likely worked on the fringes of the business. Those in the thick of it don't need to impress or drop names.

After a while, he began to run down some of the professionals he had just named, listing the reasons why they were such awful people. What he didn't know was that I was listening (it wasn't hard to do because of his volume) and, furthermore, that I knew most everyone he was berating. I chose not to say anything, but this guy certainly left an impression on me that I won't easily forget. As for his date, she had probably already figured out that he was full of baloney! If he was trying so hard to impress her on a first date, why did he take her for a burger and shake, anyway?

Clients want you to be a "good hang," positive and pleasant. Recording sessions are typically quite intimate gatherings and experienced employers know that pleasant people make for a pleasant atmosphere in which to create. Be someone that your clients will want to be working closely with in the closed quarters of a studio, sometimes for many hours at a time. Even the best session singers can be replaced by someone with a more pleasant demeanor or a better attitude. Make your potential clients know that you won't rock the boat.

It is rare that you will be asked to sing on a budget solely because of your vocal prowess. Why? Your clients don't yet know your work ethic or your attitude toward working with others. You usually have to earn the trust of your clients before they will go out on a limb to spend part of their budget on you. That starts by showing them that you are courteous and possess a pleasantly appealing personality—a good hang!

Sometimes it's hard to be courteous when faced with rejection. You will hear "no thanks" often in your pursuit and even more often you won't get an answer at all. Music industry professionals are notoriously evasive. But a good attitude matters and often pays off in the job pursuit. Simply being nice just might get you in the door so that you can be heard. Ambition alone isn't enough. You need drive, but don't forget to temper your *tenacity* with *courtesy*. You'll catch more flies with honey!

(4) Tenacity. Be prepared to knock on many, many studio doors. Because you may be tempted to give up as you pursue this vocation, tenacity is probably the most important of the Six Safecrackers as you begin your career as a session singer.

Of course, there is a fine line between tenacity and being a pest. I am often asked by my students, "How long should I give so-and-so before I contact them again about a gig?" My standard answer is "one week." Studio professionals stay very busy and often don't have time to get back with you. Then they forget. A gentle reminder is always a good idea. Follow-up is mandatory to landing a studio gig. Again, be courteous. You don't want to bug them and you certainly don't want to seem desperate. Desperation is a turnoff. Always be considerate of their schedules. Ask them if they're busy at the moment before going into a long oration about how you are perfectly suited for session work.

Tenacity + courtesy = an effective combination!

Gifted vocalists are a dime a dozen in major music towns. Therefore, pursuing business relationships is key to establishing yourself in the recording industry. (See, I mentioned it again!) It's an ongoing joke among studio professionals on Music Row that "the folks back home" think that just because you're not on the radio you must not *really* be doing anything in the music business. That's so funny because there are literally thousands of music professionals who serve as spokes in the wheel that keeps the recording business turning. That's good news for you because that means there is most likely a place for you on that wheel—if you have the tenacity.

Once you get your shot at studio success, you're going to need courage. Lots of it!

(5) Courage. It will take a great deal of intestinal fortitude to make many calls before meeting the decision makers. Before you get out there, say a prayer, play the theme from *Rocky*, eat your Wheaties . . . do whatever you need to do to be courageous as you pursue this goal.

It also takes courage to set foot in the *cage*, to be willing so step up to the mic and quite literally to let your voice be heard. I have a phrase that I use frequently as I step into the vocal booth and slip on the headphones: "Are you ready for me to saddle up?" This conjures up a heroic cowboy image that I find adventurous and fun. When I'm laying down a vocal, I'm in my element, in control, confident, on an adventure and riding tall in the saddle. That image brings me courage. Another vision is Yours Truly in a major league game stepping up to the plate to smack one out of the park in the bottom of the ninth inning. So dream up your own image of courage! Psych yourself up! Again, being a session singer is not for the timid!

Once you've been invited to get behind the mic, your skin will have been toughened from some hard knocks in the marketing process, yet you will still need to tap into emotions from the depths of your heart. Being vulnerable takes courage, but you can do it! Loosen up by just "stepping in it!" Tell the engineer you want to do a run-through to get used to the track, and don't be afraid to be a little reckless and messy with it that first time through. Leave your fear outside the door of that vocal booth.

And if you just can't seem to muster the courage, remember the alternative.

A highly successful songwriter friend of mine won ASCAP's Song of the Year honors a few years ago and was asked to perform the song at the awards dinner. Although she is a wonderful singer (and once a top session singer herself), she was nervous about performing for her peers. As she was getting dressed for the event, she expressed her fear to her husband, telling him she was afraid *to perform that evening. He responded, "Think of all the times you were* afraid *you'd never have this opportunity!" That's a brilliant thought to keep in mind when fear threatens to thwart the exciting opportunities you'll be given as a recording professional.*

Saddle up—and, once you're on your way, stay committed to your dream.

(6) Commitment. It takes a firm commitment to keep trying despite the odds. It takes commitment to develop the craft, too. That's right, it's a craft—a unique style that is perfected through time yet commercial enough to satisfy your clients' goals. Anything worth doing requires sacrifice and commitment. If you're serious about becoming a studio professional, stick to your plan!

The door into the recording industry isn't easy to open. It takes more than brute force. You'll need to use all of the Six Safecrackers: Talent, Confidence, Courtesy—Tenacity, Courage, and Commitment (TCC—TCC)! You can do it if you're prepared. *Confessions* will help you with this . . . and then, it's up to you.

Now, let's define the session singer's role in the recording process.

What Exactly Does a Session Singer Do, Anyway?

Most often, a session singer falls into one of three roles: background vocalist, lead vocalist, or both.

A *background singer* is usually somewhat of a vocal chameleon, capable of changing tone and style to match the lead vocal. Most often a session background vocalist is asked to blend with the recording artist so as not to overpower the lead vocal but, instead, to add texture while harmonizing. It is a benefit, in this instance, to possess a more generic voice quality. Singers with a distinctive style are more suited for lead vocal work. A distinctive background vocal is more apt to "stick out" on the track and, thus, detract from the overall production. There are occasions when a more stylistic background vocal approach is requested in a session but it is rare. Laying down backing vocals isn't a limelight job. A background vocalist's chief responsibility is to enhance, or *blend with*, the lead vocal.

"Blending," incidentally, is a skill that's learned through experience. If you're a quick study and become good at it, you'll be asked to blend quite often on sessions. This is a valuable specialty, as you can see by looking at the *liner notes* (the credits printed inside the jewel case of most CDs); in certain genres of music, you'll see some of the same background vocalists listed again and again, often because they excel at blending their voices with the lead or other harmony vocals.

I've performed bgv's (background vocals) only sporadically throughout my career. Much more of my work has been as a lead vocalist on a wide array of projects, including publishing demos (whereby a music publisher hires a vocalist to sing new songs written by their writers), commercial jingles (whereby a jingle producer hires a vocalist to sing commercials for broadcast), reference or guide vocals for accompaniment tracks (whereby amateur vocalists can follow a vocal to learn a song for live events), and other settings. I usually add my own background vocals, since a lead vocalist is often asked to also provide bgv's to his/her lead vocal if they have the ability to do so. That isn't always the case as there are good professional background vocalists only a phone call away. However, in the studio where time is money, if an employer can have the lead vocalist also do the bgv's—hey, even better. (Or at least quicker!)

Cracking the Safe

I won't lie to you: Recording industry professionals are a tight-knit group. So even if you're a good singer, you will need some experience before you can expect to be hired for a session. Of course, the next question is, "How am I supposed to gain experience in the studio if I can't even get through the door and into the studio in the first place?" Ah, yes, the old Catch-22! Luckily, there is an answer to this dilemma . . . and the solution will actually kill two birds with one stone.

You will need a *demo* (an audio representation of your vocal work on a CD) to give to potential employers. There are ways to make this happen. Begin by doing some research to find an inexpensive recording studio where you can pay an hourly rate to record three or four songs that represent your vocal abilities well. You can find a good, affordable studio in any major music city as well as in many small towns. Software-based recording systems, such as ProTools, account for a plethora of studios located in homes and garages all across the country. Obviously, these home-based studios have very low overhead costs. In Nashville alone, hourly rates for a home studio can be as low as $25/hour as opposed to some major recording studios whose rates can be thousands per day. Some home studios are advertised. Some are not. Ask your local music store if they know of any they can recommend. Many of the stores have bulletin boards with studio business cards push pinned to them. Call the owners of these studios and ask them what they have to offer. Also, ask anyone you know in the music business if they've worked in a particular studio. Always ask the studio owner for a "demo CD" to listen to the quality of their work before jumping into the first one that sounds like a good deal.

A no-cost solution to recording a vocal demo is to check with audio vocational schools and colleges in your area that offer courses in recording engineering. These schools need "vocal talent" for their classes. Make the calls or pay them a visit. While you're there, you might also put your name and contact information on a bulletin board located in any of the schools. The heading "Free Vocalist for Sessions" will likely get either the school's or an individual student's attention. Being a guinea pig is worth it if you need a free demo. You will also be getting free studio experience!

Now you know a couple of ways to record your demo CD on a limited budget. Once you've booked your studio time, there are a few elements to consider in order to represent your vocal work effectively. . . .

BE REAL! Be realistic and work within your limits when recording your vocal demo. Your client will be sorely disappointed if you can't perform as well as the singer on your demo. Do not produce something that you can't pull off live! If you have to do a *fix* (a vocal do-over or edit) on every line of a certain song, then you probably shouldn't be recording that song. Stay true to your own unique vocal style and ability. In other words, don't try to sound like a name artist. There is value in having your own vocal style. We will discuss the importance of establishing your vocal identity in Chapter 6.

Don't "overproduce" your demo. Clients want to hear your vocal ability, not a fancy production. A guitar/vocal or piano/

vocal demo will be enough production for your potential client to hear clearly what you can do. Simple production will also save you production costs, as opposed to recording a full band demo. If you don't have access to an accompanist who is capable in the market you are pursuing, ask the studio owner for recommendations. A music store may have a list of good players as well. Make sure that your accompanist doesn't "overplay." Remember, your potential client doesn't care how well your accompanist plays. Your objective is for the decision maker to hear *you*. It's *your* demo!

SELECTING SONGS TO DEMO Potential clients such as music publishers, successful songwriters, producers, and studio pros do not have time to listen to a long demo. They might listen to three songs. In fact, unless you intend to sell your own CDs there is *never* a need to pay to record a full-length CD. Hear me now: If someone is trying to convince you to pay them to record an album's worth of songs with no marketing or sales plan in place . . . *Run!* Run like the wind! You are about to be taken to the cleaners!

Your three-song demo should include one up-tempo tune, one mid-tempo, and one ballad. You should record songs that are good examples of the genre in which you want to work. Be true to your vocal style. For instance, if your natural strength is traditional country music and it's a stretch to sing pop or rock songs, don't record a pop- or rock-flavored song, even if that is the going rage. You ultimately want to be happy with the work you're doing and it must be natural. Authenticity is essential to a great recording. You want to define your particular style so that a client who has *your kind of song* will think immediately of *you*. Remember, your vocal honesty will pay off for you. You'll sleep better, too!

Where do you find the right songs for your demo? Look for songs that fit your natural vocal style and songs that highlight your vocal strengths. Original songs are fine if you're absolutely certain that your songs are market-ready. Otherwise, choose material that a similar vocalist has already recorded (perhaps, album cuts that weren't released as a single) or ask a music publisher to send you material similar to your vocal style. For instance, if you have a Vince Gill quality to your voice, ask them for songs they would "pitch to Vince Gill." When you call them, tell them that you're putting together a demo and would like to hear some of the songs in their catalog. Smaller, independent publishers are more apt to offer you songs, so you might fare better looking up a list of publishers, perhaps via a Google search, that aren't big conglomerates like BMG or Sony. If you live close enough, tell them you'll pick up the material—possibly a good move, if that lets you meet someone at the company. Remember, anyone you meet in the industry is a potential client! When you pick up the songs, ask if you can bring them the finished demo for their feedback.

Here's a *scandalous secret* of the music industry: Everyone wants to feel important, that their opinion matters, that they've contributed to someone's future and to the industry. Asking music professionals for feedback and assistance will flatter them and help you at the same time.

TAKIN' IT TO THE STREETS When your three-song demo CD is recorded and mixed by the studio engineer, hit the streets and start knocking on doors. Let anybody that's anybody in the recording industry hear what you have to offer! Print good labels, using a good labeling software program like MediaFACE by Neato, so that your contact information is clearly visible. List your name, phone number, and email address visibly. Make sure your voicemail greeting is friendly but not silly. Be a pro!

Make plenty of copies of your CD. Call CD duplication services for prices. Many of them can also burn your information into the CD itself, if you'd prefer that to doing it yourself with the labeling software. Do not hand-write your contact information. The more professional your presentation looks, the more you will be perceived as a professional.

Offer your services at an affordable rate. It will be easier to get your foot in the studio door if possible clients know you can save them money. Once you've established yourself, you can raise your rate. You should offer a *first-time rate discount* at a very low price—something like $25/song will floor them!—as long as you're not working *on the card* at a union-regulated studio. (This refers to recording at a studio affiliated with AFTRA, the singer's union; we'll talk more about this in a later chapter.) Show them what you can do and raise your rate next time. Even if they hire you at a cheap rate but never call you back, at least you've done a paid session! (I'll show you how to build on that first paid session in the next chapter.) Well-established session singers can charge upwards of $200/song or hour, whichever comes first. You can make even more singing commercial jingles. We will talk about specific rates in a later chapter.

For now, your assignment is to record and get your voice out there! Introduce yourself to anyone you think can be helpful to you in your endeavor to be a professional session singer. Get in the door! Record at every opportunity—even if it's for free—to hone your chops while you're tracking down session work. You've got your promotional kit together and you're officially open for business! Someone will eventually call you.

Refer often to the Six Safecrackers as you begin the marketing process. This will help your confidence and your sanity.

Do your research, online, and in various publications to find out who the decision makers are in the town where you want to work. Be diligent in your pursuit. Keep going until they start saying "Yes!"

CHAPTER 2

"Politics" Isn't a Dirty Word

How to Stay in the Business

I remember my first real professional vocal session very well. It was the summer right after I graduated from high school. I had recorded in the studio before, as the lead singer of a band. We were fairly well known in Memphis and very well known among our large high school student body. Among those aware of my vocal abilities was a student who had graduated a couple of years ahead of me. She was now working as a staff writer at a commercial jingle company. At one time, she had told me that she would like me to sing a jingle for her sometime. I contacted her as soon as I graduated, and she said she had a jingle for me to try. We would see how well I did with it and go from there.

I drove my old '72 Buick LeSabre to midtown Memphis, praying the whole way there. I remember that peculiar feeling of nervousness and confidence that comes from contemplating the unknown. What if I didn't understand what someone asked me to do? What if I messed up? The questions were plentiful, but my ability, my faith, my confidence, and my courtesy were my allies.

I don't recall how smoothly the session went, but I was called back numerous times to sing quite a few more jingles. Some of them were regional, a couple were national, and many of them were "lo-cal" spots that aired in towns all over the country. I even had the opportunity to record a few spots that aired on my own local radio and TV stations. That was the first time I had ever heard my solo vocal work on the air, and it was very cool! Receiving my first pay-check as a professional studio singer was exciting. I was hooked for life. The process was inspiring, the environment was creative, and the results of my efforts were the building blocks of a wonderful and enjoyable career.

By the way, the writer friend for whom I initially sang those jingles moved to Nashville a few years before I did and became a hit songwriter. So I'll say it again: Building good business rela-tionships is invaluable. You never know where someone will end up—like the top of the charts!

In Show Biz, It's "Who You Know" (and That's Okay!)

Everything is political. If you want to move up from bagger/cashier to management at a grocery store, then you need to get to know the management! They need to get to know you as well. And this networking principle never ends: Whether you're talking groceries or demo sessions, the beginner and the seasoned pro both need to know the decision makers as they prove their worth to them.

At the beginning of a session singer's career, the best thing you can do is to tell everyone you know that you are trying to build your business. In a city like Nashville, just about every-one knows someone in the music business. The more people you can tell about your endeavors, the more likely you are go-ing to hear "Hey, I know so-and-so in the music biz who may be helpful to you!"

So how exactly do you spread the word? I'm glad you asked . . .

Make up business cards that list your name, identify you as a "session vocalist," and include your contact information. Place them in obvious places where you are most likely to find clientele: music stores, recording studios' bulletin boards (ask first), songwriting organizations—anywhere that musicians, writers, and producers frequent.

Contact music publishers, commercial jingle companies, and recording studios. Studios don't always hire the *talent* (as singers and musicians are sometimes called). Most studios allow their clients to bring in their vocalists of choice. Still, it's a good idea to begin developing relationships with studios in your area.

When you call, tell them you're a session vocalist (you are what you think you are!) and that you're looking for session work. Ask them, "Would you mind if I brought you my vocal demo?" They will most likely let you do this.

When you take your demo to them, make sure to use the courtesy and confidence we discussed earlier. Thank them for taking time to listen. Ask them if you can call them in a few days for their feedback. Go ahead and ask them to keep you in mind for upcoming sessions. Timing is everything! They may have a session coming up for which you are a perfect cast.

Keep a list of where you've taken your CDs, who you've talked to, and any conversation to which you can refer when you follow up with them. Then, make sure and call them back in—remember?—*one week*. Of course, the hope is that they will call you before the week is over, but recording professionals are busy and need to be reminded of you and your work.

Another *scandalous secret to success* in finding clients is to go to songwriters' shows in your area. At the shows, introduce yourself to writers whose material matches your vocal style. Being a fan of your client's work will give you incentive to perform your best in the studio. It's always a good thing to have a mutual admiration between your client and yourself. Give them your card and tell them you would love to sing a demo for them sometime. Getting to know the songwriting community is an excellent way to promote your work. Join free songwriting and musician organizations. Make it known that you've hung your sign out and that you're accepting any and all customers. If you sing live, pass along your card to anyone interested in your work at the venues where you play.

As you begin to pick up more sessions, *always ask for a copy of the finished recording*. When you have a few songs under your belt and you think they represent your work well, you can use the recordings to make a *scope demo* (a CD with snippets of a few songs that you've recorded, highlighting your unique vocal strengths). As you do more sessions, you will meet, work with, and get to know engineers; those with access to their own recording gear might give you a good deal on helping you put together your scope demo. You can then use your scope demo as your audio business card. Print your contact information on your scope demo, make plenty of duplications and give them to any and all potential clients. You can now strategically place your scope demo CDs in the same places you'd left your business cards, so that your potential clients can actually *hear* your work. You're making progress!

Another way to utilize any work you do in the studio is to *always ask the client if they will be a reference for you*. If you want, you can then put together a short list of references and a short *bio* (biography of yourself and summary of your work) on one sheet of paper to attach to your scope demo. Use good-quality paper and a nice rubber band to attach this sheet to your CD. Of course, the more reputable the reference, the more likely you are to get more and better work. Who you know and especially who you work with goes a long, long way in a business of perception like the recording industry. And there's nothing wrong with that. People want to work with the best in the biz!

Want a Snack or the Buffet?

People often ask me if they need to move to a city like Nashville, L.A., or New York to find work as a session singer. I tell them that all depends on how much they want to put on their plate. If you believe you'll be happy doing sessions in your hometown, and if there's enough work there to keep you busy, then stay home and be happy. There is nothing wrong with being a big fish in a small pond. If, however, you want to compete with the major-league players in a big music town, then bring your appetite. There's a lot to "chow down on" in a big recording city. There is more work in a big town but there is more competition too. Opportunities abound in Nashville and I'm glad I made the move, but there are plenty of studios in cities like Memphis, Dallas, Austin, and Chicago, too. *The Recording Industry Sourcebook*, by Thomson Course Technology, offers a good rundown on recording facilities throughout the U.S., listed geographically by regions (East, West, etc.) and specific cities.

If you hit your ceiling in your hometown, you can always begin to lay the groundwork for a move to a larger recording studio market by utilizing some of the same strategy in Chapter 1 of this book. Use your local references and your recorded work to put together an impressive promo kit for the "big boys."

Keep Your Chin Up in the Down Time!

If your efforts don't trigger immediate response, don't take it personally. Given the busy nature of the recording industry, this almost certainly has more to do with your potential clients' lack of time than your lack of talent. So don't let the "down time" get you down in the process. Instead, use it to your advantage! Spend that time honing your studio skills: Singing as often as possible to stay strong for when you do get the session call. Be ready at all times. Go to writers' shows, see a vocal coach, stay busy, press forward. Keep the faith!

Follow up often with everyone who has received your scope demo. If you're getting at least one CD into someone's hands each day, you'll be busy making follow-up calls and visits. Be persistent but not a pest.

Again, offer your services for an inexpensive fee. If you're not lining up sessions after several weeks of persistence, offer your services for free. Remember, it's about building relationships. An awesome free vocal performance on your part can have a ripple effect. If you do a superb job, your client will actually feel beholden to you. Ask them to use you again and to spread the word; tell them that's payment enough. You'll be telling the truth, because news travels fast in the tight-knit recording world! You can charge a standard fee (whatever you set in your mind that you won't go below) the next time you do a vocal for that client.

I had reached my ceiling in Memphis. When it came time to make the move to Music City, I had an arsenal of ammunition. My scope demo included lots of reputable commercial jingles and several of my own song demos. I asked everyone I knew with a connection to the recording industry if they knew the reputable jingle agencies—they're often called jingle houses—*in Nashville. I gathered information and came up with a handful of companies. I made the calls, smiled as I handed the owners my scope demo, and followed up with them a week later.*

I found freelance work with an agency that cranked out jingles like an assembly line. That was okay with me; I needed the work. I was also adding ammo to my Nashville arsenal. I was using those sessions to gain more sessions. Each studio experience was a stepping-stone. I maintained integrity even when creative differences irritated me. I was building relationships, so I let the production disagreements go. I gradually offered my suggestions for improving the recording as I earned the jingle producer's trust. More work with more jingle houses filled my calendar. I was on my way to making session work into a lucrative career!

You can do the same! Maintain your integrity as you build good working relationships. Your work ethic will gradually begin to speak for itself.

Now that you're meeting people that can help you get into the studio as a professional session singer, are you sure you're ready? You've got to be "packin' heat" if you plan to make it in the highly competitive world of the recording industry. Preparation is the key!

CHAPTER 3

Packin' Heat

The Importance of Preparation

What to Pack for Your Virgin Voyage into the Studio

Okay, you've received the call. You're about to take your first step into the vocal booth as a professional session singer. Are you prepared? Being prepared is often what separates the amateurs from the pros. An amateur assumes that you just walk into a studio, record a vocal, and just like that—you're done. Yeah, right.

Have you "packed your bags" with everything you need? If you've been recording in a home studio or any studio environment at all—if you've gone over your Six Safecrackers—if you've read this far!—you're ready to step into the studio as a pro for the first time.

Remember, the key to being as confident as possible on your virgin trip into the cage is preparation. You can't be too prepared! The more you've lived with the song(s) ahead of time, the more comfortable you will be singing it, the more conversational you will sound singing it, and the more authentic you will sound singing it. That's what will impress your client and help them sell the song!

Your work begins not *on the downbeat*, when the actual session starts, but when you *get the call* for the session. When your client calls, ask for a *worktape* (a rough audio version of the material you will be singing, usually on CD despite the antiquated name), which you will want to receive in ample time to learn the material well. Utilizing the worktape, you may need to establish what key will be the best one for you to sing in to do the best job with their song. Inform your client of the key in plenty of time so that they can relay this to the *session leader* (usually one of the session players), who will write the charts for the rest of the studio band. (You will also need to request a lyric sheet, preferably double-spaced, to be received with the worktape so that you can make notes to yourself ahead of time). I'll go into detail in Chapter 6 about specific notes you can make to yourself that will help to make the vocal session go even more smoothly.

The worktape is usually a "bare-bones" production, with a *scratch vocal* (a rough guide vocal by which you can learn the song). The song on the worktape is usually performed by the writer. (Deciphering that performance can be an art in itself sometimes!) If there is a worktape available, make it as easy as possible for your client and ask where you can pick it up. If there isn't a worktape, go into the studio with a lot of energy and be as quick a study as possible. Remember, time is money! One reason I'm asked back to sessions frequently is that I can learn the material quickly. As you do more and more sessions, you too will become quicker at learning the material on the spot.

It is important to have at least a working knowledge of *sight-reading* (the ability to read vocal music). You can learn this by taking lessons from a vocal coach. Look for vocal coaches in the Yellow Pages, or ask a local music store, where you can also buy some books to help you learn sight-reading.

Sometimes you'll be called upon to perform your own scratch vocal as a guide for the band as they *track* (record their parts). To make this easier, I also highly recommend learning the *Nashville Number System*, a kind of musical shorthand that most professional musicians use to communicate with one another while working out a new song. Once you know it, you can find your place easily in a session as the players use the system to work on specific areas of the song.

When you sing a scratch vocal, you are merely used as a guide and your volume and effects level isn't of great importance. Once the "tracking" is finished (after the band records its tracks to your scratch vocal, usually in one or two takes), you will then work on the "real" vocal, which will be on the finished recording. I'll go into more details about this a little later.

Stepping in It

Knowing studio lingo is key to good communication with your engineer and producer. For instance, you may need to ask the engineer to make the vocal "wetter" or "hotter" in the "cans." What on earth does that mean? *Wetter* means more reverb effect, or echo, on your vocal track as you're listening through your *cans* (headphones). To make the vocal *hotter* means to turn up the level of the vocal in your headphones. Your producer may ask you to *lay back in the pocket*, which means to sing just a tad behind the beat for more of a bluesy performance.

Lots of terms get bantered back and forth in the studio between engineer, producer, and session singer; you'll learn them with time and experience. For now, if something is unclear, just ask someone to explain. The clearer you are on everything, the faster the session will go.

The important thing to remember is this: establish good communication with the team in the control room (at the mixing console), just as a pilot stays in touch with the air traffic controller. Tell them what you need sonically to inspire you to give a great performance. Tell them early in the run-through of the song what your needs are, such as more vocal level or less track level, so that you all don't have to go through the entire song several times. Remember, saving time is saving money for your clients, and they'll love you for it!

The engineer will want to do a run-through to set vocal and track levels, to set reverb levels if needed and to get a feel for your tone and how well the vocal cuts through the track. This initial run-through, which I call *"stepping in it,"* is an audio icebreaker. It gives the session singer an opportunity to recklessly go through the song, perhaps, getting a little messy in the process. It loosens you up and breaks the ice for you and the engineer. The producer will get an idea of how you're going to sound on the song too. Remind the producer that you are only getting a feel for the track on this first time through so that they will know it will improve as you do another take or two. "Stepping in it" also allows you, the session singer, to find your *pocket* (on the beat, behind the beat, wherever the vocal sounds best in the groove of the track). It lets you find the tricky spots, such as lyrics that can be tongue-tanglers, or modulations (often called *mods*; a *modulation* is a key change, usually upward a half- or whole-step somewhere in the latter part of the song).

Sometimes the first *pass* (run-through) is the one the producer likes best, but this is rare, even if the vocal is good, because the engineer is often still working to get the best audio quality. A seasoned session singer knows that there is always a better performance anyway! Plus, the more familiar you get with the track, the better the vocal performance usually becomes.

Throughout this sonic tweaking process, stay in communication with the control room. After going through it once, while the engineer is still setting levels, ask the producer if anything is not sounding quite right, before you do it *in red* (record it for real). This will help break the ice between you, the producer, and everyone else in the control room. Make sure your vocal is as the producer intended. And communicate with the engineer for your audio needs. Remember, the engineer can be your biggest ally in the recording studio.

I had sung a few demos for a songwriter friend of mine, a staff writer for a large publishing company. The publisher's creative director heard the demos and asked me to sing more demos for a few of the other staff writers. The president of the company, a legendary music publisher and artist manager, was known for having a rough exterior, so I was a little bit nervous as I arrived at the studio. The engineer, who seemed to notice, struck up a conversation with me as he got the console and the mic placement together. He asked if I had ever sung demos for this man before; I replied that I hadn't. "He can be hard on singers," the engineer said. "Just do your best and enjoy yourself. I'll do my part to make this an enjoyable experience."

And so he did: When I ran through the song the first time, he had already made sure the audio was good—sweetened with a touch of reverb and the vocal mixed well with the tracks. After my first take, the hard-to-please mogul, who had, no doubt, heard it all during his many years in the music industry, ran into the vocal booth to tell me how much he appreciated my work! I had done my homework in hopes of pleasing the publisher, the writer, and all parties involved, but the gentle encouragement of the engineer helped boost my confi-

dence that day. I was asked back many times to record demos by this company, and I have the engineer, at least in part, to thank.

Size Matters!

So, arrive 10 to 15 minutes early, packin' heat. Know the material, carry an attitude of helpfulness, and *leave your ego outside the door*. This is one instance where size matters—the smaller, the better!

Once a studio vocalist or studio player believes they have nothing else to learn, they should pack up and go back to "civilian" life. Sessions are *always* a learning experience. Recording industry pros know this. As soon as we begin to get fat and sassy, newer, more improved versions of ourselves will come along. Knowing that we can be replaced is what keeps us on our toes.

In my career advisory position at an audio engineering school on Music Row, I have the opportunity to counsel young people with fire in their bellies, many of whom want to make a career of studio work in various capacities. Students from all walks of life file into my office. Some are humble and shy. Some are bright and energetic. Some are really good kids. And some, well, they think they know it all. They are in for a very rude awakening! It's part of my job to let them know that they can be replaced, assuming they ever get a chance to record in the first place. Getting that chance will mean an attitude adjustment. I recognize the swagger of those who walk through my office door as those who have been told by someone back home (probably their Mama) that they have everything it takes to conquer the music industry. While a certain amount of confidence is required to be the best, genuine humility will help to keep them working.

I learned a long time ago that I was good in the studio. I've heard the phrase "Mak, you sing your *** off" more times than I can recall. Legendary Hall of Fame songwriters, Grammy Award–winning recording artists, and contemporary hitmakers from various genres have requested specifically that I sing their demos. Even so, I learned a long time ago that I can be replaced. Everyone can. I've witnessed incredible vocalists with bad attitudes finding their work dwindling—and wondering why!—while less talented singers pick up more work than they can handle. The talented yet unemployed singers had the right stuff needed for success; they just didn't possess the right attitude!

They thought it was about them! Someone needed to tell them that it's always about the song!

Have a "what-can-I-do-to-make-the-song-better" attitude. That's another secret to success behind the mic!

The tracks have been recorded, and your client is ready for a great vocal to make the song a successful recording. You walk through the studio door and . . . then what?

CHAPTER 4

Public Enemy #1

Egos and Etiquette

What do you do when you arrive for your very first session?

I'll walk you through some proper studio etiquette so that you'll know how to handle it, from entrance to exit. You can be your own worst enemy if your approach is unprofessional; you can make great strides toward success when you practice courtesy and good studio etiquette.

In Control in the Control Room

Session times are typically 10 a.m., 2 p.m., and 6 p.m. You've arrived 15 minutes early, possibly still listening to the work-tape with your CD Walkman. (By the way, here's another secret for picking up more session work: Arrive even earlier to meet the session players. Tell them you'll be doing the vocal on what they've just played. Give them either your scope demo CD or a business card and ask them to keep you in mind as they do sessions for other clients. It isn't out of the ordinary for a player to hear a producer talk about needing a vocalist for certain material while doing a tracking session. A pro session player can be a wonderful ally. You can refer one another for certain sessions.)

You know the material you'll be singing and you've left your ego outside. Speak politely and confidently to whoever is just inside the door as you arrive for your session. Tell them you're there to sing a demo for [your client]. If there is more than one studio in the facility, ask which room your client is in and if they're ready for you. If you have to wait a few minutes, that's time to learn the song even better as you continue to listen to your Walkman. Initiate a polite conversation with whoever is in the room with you, but don't take them away from their work by being too talkative.

Someone will let you know when they're ready for you in the studio. Be humble. Be confident but not cocky. Walk into the studio and greet *everyone* in the room. You're not sure who plays what role in the session, so it's important to make a connection with everyone there. You will most likely be led to the control room. The session engineer will probably be sitting behind the mixing console, tweaking the tracks that the session players have recorded. The producer, who may or may not be the writer, will hand you a new lyric sheet. Take it, just in case there has been a lyric change since you received the first one. Ask them if there has been a lyric change. (Never assume anything in the studio. It's best to always ask questions so that you're sure of what to do. You need to be about saving the client time and money so cover all your bases. The more time you save them, the more they will want to have your services again!) Circle the new lyrics and place the sheet next to the original sheet on your music stand. If there hasn't been a lyric change, you will want to use only your original lyric sheet because it probably includes your notes. I, personally, scribble all over the sheet, so it would be difficult to transfer all of that information quickly to a new one. And *quickly* getting behind the mic is a secret to success!

Look at a new lyric sheet to make sure that the *format* is identical to what the producer and engineer are using for their references. "Format" means how the song is laid out on the page and in the production—for example, verse 1, then a chorus, then verse 2, then the chorus, then a *bridge* (some songs contain a bridge, a segment of the song that often changes melody or key, usually after the first or second chorus), then back for another chorus and a *tag*, which is usually a repetition of the last line of the chorus. (This is referred to as a "refrain" in classical music.) The engineer should also have a lyric sheet to refer to so that he or she can know where to "punch" in and out of the track as needed to fix vocal parts.

So when you receive your lyric sheet, make sure the format hasn't changed and that the lyrics haven't changed before going into the vocal booth. Remember, ask the producer anything you need to know before leaving the control room. It's okay to ask once you're in the vocal booth, but try your best to stay focused on recording once you get started. Try not to stop in the middle of a *take* (a vocal that's being recorded) to ask a series of questions; that will hamper the mood.

Getting Plugged In—Connecting with the Engineer

How well you relate to the folks in the control room will determine how well the session goes. As I mentioned in the last chapter, the recording engineer is your best ally as you get set up in the booth. More than once, engineers have helped to save the day by sticking up on my behalf when a producer has asked too much of me. They've even talked in code to me at times when a producer "just didn't get it." So it's always a good idea to do your best to hit it off with the session engineer. The time spent with the engineer in the cage will give you an opportunity to chat with them politely while making that vital connection.

As the engineer or his or her assistant checks the microphone height and its proper placement, and while they check the *popstopper* (a screen that helps eliminate the pops that letters "p" or "t" make while a vocalist is singing), they will be in the booth with you. Let *them* adjust the mic. Too many session singers, trying to move a "boom stand," wind up dropping an expensive microphone! (A *boom stand* is a mic stand with an extension that gives you room to move your arms and legs a little without bumping the stand during a recording—an impact that could leave an audible "boom" on the track.)

The engineer will also help you get the best placement for your *music stand*. This is often a sturdy black metal stand that sometimes has a small, attached lamp to help you see the lyric. The lamp is especially helpful in a vocal booth that contains a *dimmer control*. (A dimmer control can be quite beneficial in establishing an appropriate ambience to inspire a good vocal performance. I love dimmer controls!) Music stands can vary in style. You'll find wooden or flimsy silver metal stands in certain studios, but the black metal stands are most prevalent. A music stand is standard because a vocalist holding a lyric sheet can rattle the paper, making it easy to pick up on the recording. As you're getting set up in the vocal booth, place your lyric sheet and pencil on the stand.

By the way, I keep referring to the *vocal booth*, but sometimes the vocal mic will be in the middle of the studio, right in front of the glass that divides the control room from the tracking room. The engineer may feel they get a better audio quality recording that way. Still, I will refer to the session singer's domain as the "vocal booth."

I use my own pair of headphones because I know what I like. You never know what kind of headphones you will have to use in a studio session, and I'm particular about what I want sonically. Each brand has pros and cons. Some accentuate the high frequencies, others highlight the bottom end. Some of the better "cans" have a good mix of high and bottom end. Certain headphones fit more comfortably than others. It will take time and experience to decide which headphones you prefer. Once you have a good working knowledge of various headphones, you may want to purchase your own so that you don't get stuck with an inferior set. The engineer or assistant will plug your headphones via quarter-inch jacks into a *direct box*, which gives a *feed*, or audible connection, to the engineer. The engineer will show you how to get more *level* (volume) for the *overall mix* (everything that's in the cans—vocal and band tracks) as well as for the vocal mix only. Adjusting your level is usually done with a simple turn of the knob. Sometimes, the engineer will have control of the mix level, but usually you will have some control over your own headphone mix. In Chapter 6, I'll clue you in on how to get an inspiring headphone mix.

Right now, let's talk a little more about communicating effectively with the engineer and producer.

I Just Work Here

Remember, you are working with the engineer and the producer toward a common goal: a great recording! You're on the same team. Be enthusiastic about the song. The producer will appreciate your interest in making his/her song the best it can be. *I just work here* should be your mantra as you step up to the mic. You should offer suggestions *only if asked*. This applies especially to enhancing the song's lyrics or melody. After you've established a longstanding working relationship with the producer, you can begin to offer suggestions humbly. Ask, "Do you mind if I make a slight suggestion?"—but only after you've earned that right, which will take several sessions of simply doing what's asked of you. Even established session singers are careful not to overstep their creative boundaries. As you develop your reputation within the studio industry, you may be called upon for suggestions more often, but you have to build to that place of respect in your career. Until then, keep your nose down and ask yourself *what you can do to make the song better*, not *how you can best be heard*. Remember, it's about the song! Your attitude of excellence will pay off long before those who just want to *hot dog* for the attention. Your client will want you back again, once you know they care about their material.

I have my favorite writers to sing demos for. It's easy to care about great songs by some of my favorite writers. It's more of a chore to care about songs that don't really grab me. I am more se-lective about my work than I used to be, but I still run across songs that just don't move me when I'm asked to sing them. I maintain a good attitude when the song doesn't exactly knock me out, because I care about my long-term business relationship with the writer and/or producer.

At the beginning of my studio career, I was often a "professional turd polisher" (as many session singers crudely put it), doing my best to make art out of crap. I sang demos for writers who were honing their craft, just as I was honing mine, but are now writing number-one songs. Not long ago I was pleased to see one old writer friend receive his first number-one country song! We've both come a long way!

Saddle Up!

All right, you've got your headphones on, your levels are set the way you want them for peak performance, and you've run through the song a time or two (stepped in it!) while your new friend, the engineer, prepped the audio for your vocal work. It's time to do what you've known you can do well for many moons now—shut up and sing!

There is technique involved in a professional session performance. More than that, though, there is communication involved. Do you know that place between thinking about singing and actually singing? Do you know how to sing *conversationally* rather than giving a performance? Can you balance being *commercial* with being genuine?

Only the recording will tell. These elements are what separate those "who can sing" from those who are truly professional vocalists. Let's tackle these very important aspects of your vocal delivery that will make or break the song—and possibly your career.

Let's *saddle up*!

CHAPTER 5

Premeditated Murder

Technique-ing the Life Right Out of a Song

I was once asked to sing a few demos for a great songwriter who had written one of the most memorable songs of the 1980s and was still writing great stuff in the 1990s. I learned the songs and knocked them out like clockwork. Everyone was excited about my work. Well, almost everyone.

I received a call the next day from the writer. "Mak, would you be willing to come in and re-sing a couple of the songs you did for me yesterday?" he asked. "Sure, but what's the problem? I thought you loved what I did," I replied. "It was perfect, Mak, and that's the problem!" The problem is, he wanted me to sing them "worse"! The vocal wasn't rough enough around the edges, he explained. I did a re-sing for him (at the writer's expense), and while he was pleased, he never called me back for a hard-edged vocal again. Other session singers do that a lot better than I do. My style has always been smooth and soulful. Hey, what can I say? I'm a lover, not a fighter!

I still have a great deal of respect for this wonderful writer and I believe the feeling is mutual, but we both learned lessons that day.

He learned about the value of correct casting, and I learned how wise it is to stay within my strengths as a session singer.

Note to Writers: From the Other Side of the Glass

Hey, songwriters and producers—I love you guys! You are my true brothers and sisters. Still, you need to hear some preachin'. I've come to the studio experience with your perspective, as a songwriter myself. I've spent countless hours producing my song demos, whether singing them myself or casting other vocalists to sing for me.

Writers, casting the right vocalist is so very important when recording a demo. You don't want to bring in a singer and tell him to "sound like Garth Brooks"! Choose a singer whose vocal qualities are similar to Brooks, or whoever your model is, but allow him to stay within his own comfort zone. A good working relationship with a writer/producer begins when he or she tells me to "sing it like *you* would sing it!" I cast session singers based on how I want the song to sound when production is finished. If I write a rockin' country song for a female, I know just who to call. If I write a more contemporary pop–feeling song for a younger artist, I know just who to call.

Now, I realize that not all songwriters know just who to call. If not, it's very important that you do your homework to cast the right singer for your song demo. Search in various places: Ask studio managers, songwriters, songwriting organizations, performing rights organizations (ASCAP, BMI and SESAC), or AFTRA (the singers' union). If you're in a smaller town, ask local music stores or studios who they would recommend for a "Trisha Yearwood-esque" or a "Josh Grobin-esque" vocal, whatever you need. Finding and hiring the right singer for your song can make your song soar.

You'll never get that thing off the ground by using the wrong singer for your song!

If you've found a seasoned pro, let them sing! Don't over-analyze every syllable. If the session singer's phrasing or melody is a variation of the way you wrote it, don't immediately dismiss it. (By the way, *phrasing* is the rhythm or timing of the lyric as it lies in a particular line.) Be open to a studio vocalist's interpretation. After all, they're in the trenches every day, digging out the most commercial presentation possible from many rough worktapes. A session singer's variation on the phrasing, or even a slight melodic change, might just take the song to a more marketable place. Knowing when to give slack and when to draw in the reins is a large part of the creative process.

The *professional* songwriter casts the right singers and lets them do their thing with very little coaching or tweaking. It is the *amateur* songwriter who can often pick a vocal to death—literally, pick *the life* right out of a song by having the vocalist do fixes on every phrase! There must be *flow* to good creativity. Stopping to fix every word can ruin a much-needed nuance. Listen to me, fellow song crafters: Most of the time, an imperfect vocal with the right amount of emotion (not too much, not too little) is far better for the song than a perfect vocal performance with no emotion.

Bottom line: Cast the right vocalists and let them sing!

If a "bad cast" nonetheless happens, a session singer might still save the day by suggesting someone better suited for the gig. If a songwriter asks me to sing a traditional country song, for instance, I would offer to recommend a real traditional country vocalist. Likewise, if a colleague is asked to sing something more contemporary or soulful, he might suggest that the writer call me instead. Singers: It might not seem wise to pass on a session, even if you know you're not the best candidate for that particular job. But if you make a good recommendation, the writer/producer may just recall your integrity the next time *you're* the right vocalist for their song. Remember, real pros do it for the good of the song, not for a fast buck! Invest integrity into your career. It will pay off in the long haul.

Here's a quick rundown for you, songwriters:

1 Make sure your well-cast session singer has an audible CD of the song ahead of time. (You'd get a kick out of some of the tapes and CDs I've had to figure out!)

2. Make sure the CD comes with a legible lyric. (You'd also get a kick out of some of the scribbled lyric sheets I've had to figure out!)

3. Double-space the lyric so that the singer can make notes and/or "write numbers" easily. (Session singers will sometimes write their own number charts, with each number representing a note in the scale. For instance, in the key of C, "1-2-3" would be C-D-E, the first, second, and third notes in the C scale. You can learn this system with help from many pro vocal coaches.)

4. Bring lyric sheets for yourself, the engineer, and the session singer—and *make sure all three sheets are identical*. Make sure the song is *finished* before having the session singer come in to sing. Again, you'd be surprised at how many songs are still being written while a vocalist is idling in the vocal booth. Remember, session singers *charge for their time*. Long ago, I began charging per hour or per song, whichever came first. This means that while the co-writers are in the control room, arguing over a lyric, and I'm just twiddling my thumbs, waiting for them to finish, I don't lose out on the income I might have earned by doing another session during that down time.

5. Finally, know the difference between holding too tightly onto a song and allowing the studio pros to make it more commercial. Most professional session singers and players work on a daily basis to bring out the hit potential of the material they record. Sometimes it's best to let go a little bit and let these guys mold your "baby" into a moneymaker for you!

I often wonder if songwriters who won't loosen their grip on their song would be better off just recording it themselves . . . .

Not long after I moved to Nashville, a very successful composer in the Christian music field asked me to sing demos for him. He was an excellent song craftsman and very meticulous about how he wanted his songs demoed. He usually sang his own demos and then took them straight to the artist that he wrote most of his material for in that era. So when he started working me to death, asking me to tweak every phrase or even every syllable, it occurred to me that he would probably have been better off singing his own demos rather than trying to make me sound just like him. Eventually, I chose not to subject myself to that torture anymore! I liked the guy and admired his writing but, for the good of the song, he should have stuck to singing his own demos. Maybe he did from then on.

Note to Writers: What to Expect from Your Session Singer

You can expect your session singers to know your song(s) reasonably well when they step up to the mic. They may or may not have every note and phrase down verbatim, but they should be pretty doggone close. One way to subtly check to see if they've done their homework is to glance at their lyric sheets. They should have made plenty of handwritten notes, there, while learning your song.

Your session singers should come to the studio with a good attitude of helpfulness and carrying no ego with them.

They should be able to communicate their audio needs to the engineer, to maximize their performance of your song.

Good vocal quality can be expected from your vocalist. If a vocalist is sick, stopped up, or hoarse, he or she should call you at least 24 hours ahead of time so that you can make other arrangements. Of course, if this is definitely the singer you want for this particular song, you might consider postponing the session until he or she feels better, but this depends on your relationship with your vocalist and whether there is a deadline.

You can expect your session singer to add life and emotion to your song and to interpret and communicate your song well. If they're unsure about the mood you want to communicate, encourage them to ask questions.

And your session singers should lay down a lead vocal track in two or three takes, which can then be edited as needed, with only a few minor fixes. You may need to adjust your singer's interpretation or phrasing early into the session (not on the first run-through, however). Making sure your vocalist knows your needs early will speed up the recording process.

You can also expect a background (or harmony) part from the demo singer if needed, but keep in mind that it's easy to overproduce a vocal. Less is usually best in a demo production. One background vocal is often all you need, even if the song seems to beg for another part. The record producer can always add more parts later on, within the record label's budget. Still, if you really feel that the song wouldn't be complete without a second harmony part, then do it.

My suggestion, though, is that you save yourself studio time and cost and try not to overproduce the vocal. Ask the session singer to sing on a line where you're not sure a harmony part should be placed. You can always *wipe that track in the mix* after the vocalist is gone and off the clock. ("Wipe that track off the mix" refers to the engineer omitting the harmony part on lines where you don't need it. Do this while your engineer is mixing your song, not when the session singer is still in the booth on your dime. A vocalist usually has a higher fee than the engineer's hourly rate.)

(Incidentally, for those new to the recording process, the sequence is: tracking first, with the band laying down its tracks; then any *overdubs*, where additional instrumental parts such as a fiddle or saxophone are recorded; then lead vocals; then background vocals . . . and then your engineer mixes the entire project, with your supervision.)

Writers, this is a *demo*, not the record. A good song should stand on its own, without the need for overly fancy production. That's the *record* producer's job. Don't take it away from them! I have heard my vocal licks completely *copped* (copied) by a radio artist and thought, "Man, I only made my session fee—I wonder what he's making for doing the same thing I did!" It's true, some producers *do* just copy the demo production, but you still don't want to overdo the vocal parts.

There is also the possibility of over-singing the lead part. Make sure your session singer doesn't go overboard. Make sure that you hold the reins when a singer is doing *too* good of a job—No kidding! A good vocal can intimidate the very artist to whom you're pitching your song.

I had written a song that I sang myself in the studio. The song was picked up by a major country artist at the time. He was excited about it, the label was excited about it, and I was thrilled! In fact, I was told that the song would be the title cut from the album! But when the artist went into the studio to record the song, he found that it had more range *(high and low notes) than he remembered. He recorded the song anyway, and I thought it was* in the can *(a done deal and on the record) . . . until I received a call a couple of days later, saying it was a no-go. Apparently, the artist decided that the song would be too hard to sing every night in concert because of its range.*

I was disappointed, but there would be more opportunities to have songs cut (recorded by a recording artist). I learned a valuable lesson, however, both as a songwriter and as a session singer. It's important to write and demo songs that most artists can sing comfortably enough not only on their records but in concert as well.

There is much to be said for hiring a session singer who has a generic vocal quality that will easily translate your song to a variety of artists without intimidating them. Honestly, I've missed out on doing some session work because I'm more of a stylist. It's your preference whether you wish to hire more of a vocal stylist or more of an all-purpose vocalist when producing your demo.

To sum up, writers, you can expect a session singer to be quick and to be as good as or better than you had hoped. Producing the vocal for your song should be a satisfying and enjoyable experience for you. After all, you're paying for it!

Okay, back to the vocalists . . . .

Effective Vocal Communication

As you slip the headphones on and adjust your lyric sheets, keep this in mind: A successful vocal session is less about *singing* than it is about *communicating well*. It is less about technique than it is about flow. It is less about performance than it is about having a sincere conversation through song with your listener. It is about balancing emotion with commercialism. Most of all, a successful vocal session is about—let's say it together—*the song*.

WELL, TECHNICALLY YOU'RE RIGHT, BUT . . . How many times have you heard someone say, "That singer's *technique* really moves me?" On the contrary, it's much more often said, "That *song* really moves me!" That is your goal as a session singer. Your client wants their *song* to move the listener. There will be wonderful writers/producers who will want you to succeed and encourage you to put your own unique vocal style into the song. Take advantage of their kindness, but continue to make it your goal to enhance their song, not overshadow it. They will have you back time and time again if you keep that attitude.

One of the reasons learning the song(s) before the session is so important is that it gives you an opportunity to live with the material, to make it your own. Of course, there is a delicate balance between making it your own and keeping it commercial. When you've gone through a couple of vocal takes, your client will let you know if you're walking that line effectively or not. You may need to pull in the reins a little—or your client may be perfectly satisfied with your interpretation. To save the client time and money, ask them, while you're still in the control room, if you may have a little creative license with their song. Most seasoned writers will know the benefits of allowing you to have some freedom with the interpretation. They can always adjust your execution, if needed, once you run through it for them.

Living with the song(s) ahead of time also gives you *mental flow*. Mental flow is that pleasurable place where you're free to "just sing" and interpret without the shackles of thinking too much, where you're not concerned so much about reading the lyric or finding your phrasing, where you're not caught up in your technique. Being concerned with technique stifles real and honest vocal creativity. Mental flow is that place where you're free to create an inspiring vocal that will move the listener. Good preparation is the key to the singer's drug—mental flow, dude!

EMOTIONAL BALANCE In a corporate office setting, employees are usually asked to leave their emotions at home. Not so in the studio—behind the mic, vocalists are expected to bring a bag full of them! As a session singer, you will need to pull out the ones you'll need to convey the song's intentions. Use moderation, but also tap into your deepest feelings when doing a vocal. A sure sign of a novice vocalist is singing in an overly dramatic fashion. Finding and executing that balance between emotion and commercialism is the mark of a professional demo singer. You will find that balance with time and experience behind the mic. Overly dramatic or overly silly vocals take away from the song itself and can be a hindrance to the listener. Record executives who will be listening to the *song* for their artists (notice I didn't say "listening to the *singer*") prefer to draw their own conclusions about the intent of the song without having a theatrical vocal thrust upon them. Having to endure an overly theatrical vocal can actually make listeners feel insulted, as if you think they can't figure out the meaning of the song without a *vocal cartoon*. These record execs are used to hearing songs presented with a certain "familiarity." Don't stray too far from the "norm" when doing your vocal. By not compromising, distorting, or overwhelming the material, you'll actually impress these execs more than you would by calling too much attention to yourself with a performance.

KEEPING IT CONVERSATIONAL This brings me to my next point. If you don't take in anything else I say about your work in the studio, listen to this: The job of a session singer isn't to give a good *performance*. What? You read it right! Your job isn't to *perform* well. It is to *give* well. It is to have a *conversation* with your listener. Sincerity, not performance, will draw your listener in. A good *performance* will cause the listener to say, "Wow, what a great singer!" A *sincere conversation*, however, will cause the listener to say, "Wow, what a great song! And who is that singer?"

One of the benefits of becoming a session vocalist working for great songwriters, publishers, and producers is that your vocal work lands on the desks of top record executives in the music industry without your having to clamor for their attention. This accounts for many of the recording artists, particularly in country music, who have been "discovered." When label execs hear a vocalist who knows how to communicate well with a listener, not just a vocalist who performs well, they just might ask, "Who's the singer?"

I had been singing some for staff writers with Sony/ATV Tree Music Publishing when the VP of Sony Productions took notice of my vocal work. He was a successful writer who, I suppose, recognized something worth marketing in my vocal work. With the help of my entertainment attorney (they're the ones who really make deals happen in the music industry), I was offered a deal to record a few sides with the company's budget. I told them "Yes."

At the same time, I was singing demos of songs I had written and some for staff writers with another publishing company owned by a successful producer. The creative director (CDs make decisions regarding song demos as well as managing the song catalog and the writing staff) played my work for the owner/producer and he, too, asked, "Who's the singer?" He, too, thought my vocal work was worth marketing. He offered me a production deal with his company, too—and, again, I said "Yes!"

Although agreeing to both deals could have led to an embarrassing situation, it worked out perfectly: The two producers were old college buddies and had wanted to produce a project together for a long time. So it worked out well.

Several other producers have offered me similar deals throughout the years I've been a session singer—all without any pressure from me. You will likely encounter similar situations if you keep your nose down and do your best with the demos you're given to sing.

Producers often ask session singers to make their vocals *conversational*. What they're really saying is, "You're singing too much and communicating too little." *Yeah*, you're thinking, *but I'm there to sing!* That's partly true, but you're there mainly to connect with the listener. Making it more "conversational" is singing the lyric more like you would say the lyric.

I'll say it again: A great vocal is more like a sincere conversation than a performance. A great performance can overshadow the song you're helping your client to market. A sincere conversation can only enhance your client's song's marketability.

YOUR OWN VOCAL STYLE Working behind the mic is a great way to establish your own vocal style. The more sessions you do, the more you will hone your unique vocal identity. This makes it easier to pursue other recording opportunities with more confidence in who you are on tape. You will learn your vocal strengths and improve your vocal weaknesses. Your range will improve with experience, as will your phrasing, your *meter* (timing or rhythm), and your vocal quality. You will learn when to use your *head voice* (singing falsetto) and when to use *full voice* (singing loudly, rather than with your head voice, to reach high notes). You will develop trills and nuances that are distinguishably your own. And clients will seek you out *specifically* because of all that you've learned about vocal performance through doing sessions. Many in the music industry know my voice immediately because I've used my time and experience in the studio to craft the ability that the Lord gave me. Most music industry professionals recognize the seasoned session singers when they hear them. You will be easily recognized, too, if you keep at it!

For new writer/producers, the rule of thumb for pitching to genders goes like this: You can usually pitch a male vocal to either a male or female artist, but you usually have better results pitching a male vocal only to a male artist. I had co-written a song that I heard as a female-artist pitch. I was busy doing demo work of my own when that particular song was going to be demoed, so my co-writer produced the demo herself. When I heard it, I was floored! It was so heartfelt, perfectly balanced between emotional and commercial, and so I asked the same question that many record execs ask: "Who's that singing?" Unfortunately, my co-writer had moved back to the West Coast and I couldn't reach her by the time I wanted—needed—to know who that singer was.

It took me a couple of years, but finally I found her! I was asked to sing a duet with this same vocalist and, voilà, it hit me who she was. This wonderful session singer, Juli Maners, and I are good friends now. And any time I have the opportunity to work with her or hear her on other demos, I am reminded of just how important it is to develop your own style. (I'm also reminded of how good she is!)

Okay, you've got the principles for singing well for your music industry client. You're in the studio, ready to "go red." You know the material. Get in the zone. Don't think too much. Remember, *mental flow, dude!* Rock on! . . . Sorry, I got a little carried away.

Next, as we get on with the session, I will discuss voice care, specific microphone technique, and certain gear that will enhance your work.

CHAPTER 6

Being "The Ringer"

Voice 101, Mic Technique 101, Gear 101

Voice 101

Professional session guitarists are extremely careful with their instruments. They don't expose them to the elements. They don't apply harsh chemicals to them. Most of the pro players I know are almost neurotic about taking proper care of their moneymakers. You know where I'm headed with this, don't you?

As a session singer, your voice is your instrument. It is your responsibility to take as good care of your instrument as all pro players take care of their instruments. Elements and chemicals can affect your instrument just as much as a musical instrument. Even more: A voice cannot be replaced once it is ruined.

There are several ways to keep your instrument in the best shape possible, but the number one secret to good vocal care is a four-letter word: *rest*. Straining your vocal cords when you're tired is not only harmful to them; it also decreases your vocal quality and your ability to focus well. I know great singers who take naps between sessions to stay fresh for the next one.

Keeping your throat lubricated is important to your vocal cords' health, too. Room-temperature or lukewarm water, which the studio often provides, is best: *room-temperature* because cold water shrinks the vocal cords, which keeps them from relaxing and hampers your range; *water* because soda is syrupy and affects vocal quality. Prescription-only throat lubrications are available, containing witch hazel and other ingredients for combating temporary (non-chronic) hoarseness, but they should be used only on rare occasions, as they can be addictive. There was a famous band whose singers actually had to take time off to "detox" from vocal lubricators. Installing a humidifier in your home to keep your cords moist is a better idea. Central heat and air without a humidifier can dry out your cords too much. The best aids to good vocal care are both natural and cheap: rest and water!

Of course, there are things to avoid that will harm your vocal work. Alcohol, cigarettes, drugs, and caffeine will dry out your vocal cords. Antihistamines and, believe it or not, many cough drops (containing menthol) will do the same. Avoid dairy products on session days as they can "gunk up" in your throat, causing you to lose some vocal control. Keeping your throat warm with a scarf on cold days is a good idea. Talking excessively decreases your vocal quality as well. Some top recording artists are instructed by their management not to talk for hours, especially before a performance.

Just use common sense and be aware of things that can be harmful to your instrument if you want it to last.

A few years ago I was becoming hoarse easily and my voice quality was decreasing with each session. In desperation, I took my problem to the Vanderbilt Voice Center in Nashville. The doctors there, just a few blocks from Music Row, do a big business taking care of many vocalists. Pictures were taken of my vocal cords, and it was determined that I had an abrasion on one of them. I didn't drink or smoke; I thought I was taking good care of my voice. Then it hit me! I was taking diet pills—supposedly all-natural—that contained ephedrine, which I have known to damage the vocal cords, hearts, and general health of several of my contemporaries. I decided that I could still work even if I had a few extra pounds on me, so I stopped the pills. I regained vocal control and my voice regained the smooth quality my clients had come to count on.

Most session singers can listen back later to something they've recorded and say, "Man, I had a cold that day!" I am often asked about remedies for a sore throat or a stopped-up nose. I'm no doctor, but I can tell you some remedies that work best for me. The same four-letter word I used earlier—*rest*—is the best remedy. But if you can't find the time to rest, here are remedies I've found that work for me.

For a scratchy sore throat, I recommend honey or syrup with or without hot decaf tea. The sugar doesn't cure anything, but it coats your throat so that you can get through the session in as little pain possible.

For a glandular sore throat, I've found that only a pain medicine such as acetaminophen or ibuprofen can get you through until your doctor can prescribe an antibiotic.

Okay, this is kinda gross, but the best way to avoid a stopped-up nose or any allergy problem, according to a pharmacist friend and my allergist, is to wash out your nose with salt water when showering. If you're already stopped up, a long, hot shower—or hot, spicy food—works pretty well. A nasal spray such as Afrin works well for the short term to help you breathe better. If you have a big session, an allergist or your doctor may prescribe a steroid for you for short-term relief.

Emotional disorder and self-esteem issues can sometimes affect your vocal quality and delivery as well. Singing professionally is akin to pro sports. A positive mindset is a secret to success. There may be a time when you need to see a counselor to work through emotional issues. There's nothing wrong with that, and it happens more often than most pros care to admit. Professional therapists are available that specifically address these types of issues.

Mic Technique 101

Three-quarters of session success is knowing how to work the microphone. Like anything else, this skill will increase with experience. For now, I can give you some pointers to help you have a successful vocal session. Let's start at the beginning.

First of all, make sure that your music stand containing your lyrics is well lit and easily seen. I like to set the stand to the right of the mic boom stand at eye level. That keeps me from straining my neck down to a lower level and therefore affecting the consistency of my volume level. Make sure your notes are made dark enough to be seen clearly with the stand's built-in light. Begin approximately six inches away from the microphone. Even though the popstopper is in place between the singer and the mic, I still slightly turn my head when singing "p," "t," or even "s" words. If that occasional consonant pop sneaks in, you will need to re-sing the word. Staying on top of that possibility ahead of time by, once again, doing your homework will help save time and money for your client.

The engineer will tell you if you're in good proximity to the mic and how you can adjust. I keep my front foot in the same place the whole time I'm doing a vocal so that my proximity stays just about the same. This is important when doing a fix—a vocal edit—on a line or a word because you'll want the new vocal to match the original vocal in volume. You'll learn to do this better with each session.

Tell your engineer what you need in your cans. I prefer the track to be a little hotter than my vocal when I'm singing. This helps me to stay in pitch easier because I have the tonic notes to rely on to keep me from wavering off pitch. If there are *overdubbed instruments* (instruments added after the initial rhythm tracks are laid down) such as a sax or a steel guitar, you may want to have the engineer omit them from your headphone mix, because they can cause you to lose pitch. Bass, piano, and guitars should all be in good pitch. Rely on them. I also prefer to have a little reverb ("a little wet") to enhance the vocal sound in my cans. Some vocalists prefer to cut their *flat* (with no reverb) and find that it keeps them *honest* (on pitch). The results will be the same once the engineer mixes the vocals, anyway. I just find that the reverb gives me a little more "inspiration" as I do my vocal. The engineer may ask you if you prefer to "cut wet or flat." I always say "just a little wet," though that's only my preference.

The engineer will adjust your volume, but you can make his or her job easier by paying attention to dynamics. You will need to come in closer to the mic on those hard-to-reach low notes and back off while belting high notes. You will also help the engineer by being quiet on the *intro* (the music track prior to when the vocal begins) and on *turnarounds* (the music between parts of the song, often between the first chorus and second verse). The less time the engineer has to spend cleaning up your messes, the quicker the session will go.

As for background vocals, a few mic techniques can help this process go smoothly.

I usually ask the engineer to give me a headphone mix with the background parts about 3/4 as hot as the lead vocal. This ratio is the same principle as the track-to-vocal ratio in that keeping the lead vocal hotter serves to keep me on pitch better. Cutting the vocals this way also gives me a better idea of how the final mix will sound, because background vocals are mixed to a lower volume than the lead.

Phrasing is key when cutting a background part. If you're unsure exactly how your lead vocal phrasing was on a certain line, ask the engineer to play it back for you before jumping in with the background part. Guessing and missing the phrasing a few times will take longer than simply listening to the lead vocal part once before nailing the background part.

A secret to nailing a background vocal quickly is to eliminate the "s" when matching up phrasing. When the "*esses*" aren't together on the lead and background vocal track, it's very noticeable. Keeping your "s" silent is a key to a quick background vocal!

Remember, a background vocal is just that—background— and doesn't require the same intensity when sung. You will find just the right sweet spot when recording background parts over time. Some session singers specialize in background parts. Be patient with yourself as you work on this skill.

Avoid making any sounds other than singing. Tapping your foot, hitting the popstopper with a ball cap, accidentally kicking the music stand, shuffling lyric sheets (that's why a music stand exists), sniffing, and even a grumbling stomach—the mic will note and dutifully capture all of these.

Believe me, once you've done enough sessions, you won't have to think about these things so much. It's like learning manners: If you learned them as a kid, you probably don't think about them now; you just *have* them.

As you can see, being a studio professional involves more than just stepping behind the mic and belting out a song. Each session is a chance to improve your work. That's what keeps this business exciting!

NOTES ON NOTES I've mentioned the importance of preparation to session success. Making notes is the key to effective preparation. Many vocal trainers can teach you standard ways to make notes using Nashville Numbers. My shorthand notes to myself are probably different from those of other session singers. Sometimes I utilize numbers, but most often I take time to learn the melody before the session and opt not to use them. Instead, I'll use my own made-up markings to help me through a song. An effective shortcut I use is to underline the lyrics where the downbeat falls. For instance, in the line "Amazing grace, how sweet the sound," the downbeat falls on "maz," "grace," "sweet," and "sound" as you're keeping rhythm. These marks help me keep my place as I sing with the track.

Still, knowing the Nashville Number System can be helpful, even if you don't mark every note. I often write "5" or "1" at the end of a line to know where to land melodically, based on the chord used by the band, with arrow marks to indicate whether the melody goes up or down. To make that clearer, a chorus will usually resolve *back to the I* (back to the main key in which the song was written); a V chord is often the last chord of a verse leading into the chorus, though not always.

Learning songs for sessions will become easier each time you make your notes. Whatever markings work best for you, though, be sure to make them in pencil where you can see them clearly. (The studio usually provides the pencil, but it doesn't hurt to bring one with you.) A pen is too permanent in case you need to "adjust the adjustment."

Gear 101

As you do more session work, you will discover certain headphones, reverbs, microphones, and even pencils that work best for you. Session singers have their own individual preferences in each case. Briefly, let me tell you some of the difference in specific gear.

If you prefer to hear your mix with more of a *high-end* (more treble) sound quality, Sony headphones will serve you well. If you desire audio with more *bottom end* (more bass), then Fostex T-20s or the even bassier T-40 headphones may be suitable. I own a pair of Fostex T-50 cans because they embody both a high-end and bottom-end sound. At first, use whatever headphones the studios have to offer you until you become familiar with various kinds. You will then be better able to decide on your preference. At that point, you may want to invest in your own pair of favorites rather than taking a gamble that the studio will have them.

If you want a little reverb on your vocal, the engineer will likely have a plethora of settings: *small room, large room, concert hall*, etc. Experience will help you discover which setting you prefer, though your decision will be based in part on the kind of song you're recording. Ask the engineer what he or she has to offer in the way of reverb effects and, if there is time, if they can let you try a few of them as you're doing your first run-through.

Knowing which microphone works well for you can be a plus. For instance, a very nice, large, and expensive Neumann U 67 or U 47 mic can excel at making your voice sound warmer, depending on your individual vocal characteristics. Other popular vocal mics include the AKG C 12 and the Telefunken ELAM-251; for female vocalists, the Neumann M 269 sometimes works well. Again, in time, you'll discover which mic works best for you.

Engineers may ask you which mic seems to work best for you; your response will suggest something to them about your vocal characteristics before you even open your mouth to sing and give them an idea about how to set certain levels to get a jump start on the vocal mix. The engineer will also have good suggestions about the right mic for you, based on the timbre of your voice.

Most studios also stock a selection of *outboard gear* (equipment that is plugged into the mixing console), including mic preamps, equalizers, and compressors; the engineer may want to try two or three of each on your vocal to see which works best. You may need to sing through the song a couple of times before he or she makes final selections. Remember, engineers work hard to make you sound as good as possible. Do your best to be patient and to form those important alliances with them.

One other piece of gear worth considering—or maybe not, depending on your preference and ability—is the *vocal auto tuner*. You need to know about it whether you agree with its use or not. To some studio veterans, never have harsher words been spoken than "That'll tune!" I tend to agree, though some maintain that it saves money in the long run. Their point is that in the time a vocalist takes to re-sing a line to correct pitch they could have long since moved on and just "auto-tuned" the line in the mix. (Ah, the almighty dollar strikes again!) The auto tuner makes me a little uneasy, knowing that mediocre and even bad singers can record a decent-sounding vocal and diminish the hard work I've put in to perfect my pitch. Is it another step closer to eliminating the need for a good session singer or not? After some experience with the tuner, I've been enlightened to the fact that although auto tuning can fix pitch it can't replace emotion. In fact, it can reduce it. A slightly imperfect vocal possessing heartfelt emotion is still worth ten times as much as a sterilized vocal. So I guess I'm in business for a little while longer and the future is still bright for new session singers like you who have the goods.

The first time a producer said to me, "That'll tune," I was appalled. I asked him what he said. He repeated, "I said, 'That'll tune.' We'll just fix it in the mix." I suppose I come from the old school where the singer sings well or finds a day job. I replied adamantly, "No, I'll re-sing it!" He explained that it would be quicker just to keep forging ahead with the song and just have the engineer fix it later. Although my feathers were somewhat ruffled by the producer's comment, and I still prefer not to use this kind of vocal enhancer, I do understand the need to save time and money. I've settled on the old adage "Everything in moderation" and made it my goal to make the producer say, "Mak, with you, we don't need the tuner!"

Your Sweet Spot

If you make each session a learning experience, you will make great strides toward a successful career. Taking good care of your instrument, working the mic, learning nuances that make you a unique and valuable vocalist, learning what gear works best for you, and striving for excellence in your work will make you successful. One day, you will step behind the mic, lock into a groove with the track, knowing just what you need to sound your best, and find that you're in your *sweet spot*—that place where you're at peak performance and you know just how to use your voice at its maximum potential. You'll realize it as you're *going down* (at the time you're recording your vocal) and you'll have the confidence to continue up the ladder of success.

Once you're in the sweet spot, you can't rest on laurels, though. You must still work hard to do the best vocal work possible for your client. Singing well is important toward a successful session. *Listening* well is just as important.

CHAPTER 7

Tracks, Lies, and Audiotape

How to Listen

There is a sense of satisfaction in a job well done. Once you've laid down your vocal track, you will have the opportunity to *listen down* (hear what you've just recorded) and the producer will mark certain spots that you may need to re-sing. It's a good idea to make your own marks on your lyric sheet as well. Keep an "I can do it better" attitude—but don't go overboard with it. Session singers sometimes overanalyze their tracks, so be careful not to take up precious studio time by being too picky. Remember, time is money in the studio. Still, point out anything you might improve on that the producer misses. Let the producer go through his or her fixes first, and then offer your suggestions to make the vocal better. They will appreciate your desire that the song be well presented.

On the other hand, be willing to let it go if the producer likes the performance as is. Always yield to his or her opinion if at all possible; though if you absolutely feel that your vocal work would be compromised, ask politely if you can do it again.

I have to admit that I'm seldom, if ever, completely happy with my work. Once I asked a producer if I could re-sing a line and he

seemed surprised: "You've got to be kidding, Makky, that was per-
fect!" Actually, it wasn't technically perfect, although it had the
right emotion, so I begged him to give me another crack at it before
giving up. I apologized profusely for taking everyone's time with
the line. He replied with a sly grin, "It's okay, I saved the original
pass"—another word for "take"—"because I knew you couldn't
top it!" He was right!

Once More with Feeling

Sometimes an inexperienced songwriter/producer will ask you
to sing a song section or the entire song many times with total
disregard to the time and expense. (Again, make the stipula-
tions of your fee clear and upfront). If you've done the best job
possible and are asked to re-sing it numerous times anyway,
there does come a point when enough is enough. The money
you're making taking so long with the writer will be good, but
the vocal will be lacking energy and quality after awhile. Tell
them that in the best interest of the song presentation, you
think it's time to set it aside for now. If you'd like to re-sing it
on another date then ask if you can reschedule. It's still about
the song, but you also have to care for your voice.

Sessions can be long and tedious. To keep your energy and
enthusiasm for the material you're recording, you might want
to take fruit or a non-chocolate energy bar with you to the
studio. Your writer/producer will likely agree that for the good
of the song you need to "take five" to rejuvenate yourself. Im-
patience as well as hunger can creep in making you irritable.
Do your best to keep your frustration in check. Take a *short*
break if you need one.

Do your best to accept critique well from your client. This
isn't always easy, but keep in mind that the critique is not

meant to be negative about your work. It is merely about making the song as strong as possible for the marketplace. Accept advice graciously from those who have been in the recording industry longer than you've been doing sessions. Stash the critiques away and apply them as necessary for the next session. Remember, this is a learning process.

Now, Listen Here!

The recording doesn't lie. It can, however, trick you, depending on your vantage point. Listening through your headphones in the vocal booth is all fine and good but you can get a totally different perspective from listening in the control room. Speaker variance and settings can make the recording sound differently from room to room. I always try to go into the control room to listen to my work. It allows me to listen for anything I might have missed when simply listening through the cans. It also gives me a better idea of what my client is hearing. The headphone mix may or may not be the same mix they're hearing in the control room.

You'd be surprised how much a different listening vantage point can change the way you're hearing your work. You may want to change your approach to the song once you've listened in a fresh environment. Sure, you want to save your client money, but don't be afraid to ask to do a vocal again if you absolutely need to for the good of the song presentation.

Once you've listened well and marked your spots, it's time to make your fixes.

Fixes

As you've listened down, your producer and you have both marked spots that you need to fix. In this digital age, there is no longer wait time for tape to rewind; the engineer will

cue the spot where you need to re-sing the line. Most engineers still call the few seconds before you come in "roll
time," even though the term refers to tape rather than to
digital technology. *Roll time* allows you time to lock into
the groove again and to match the level and the energy you
had on the first take. You will hear the few seconds of roll
time, and then the engineer will "punch in" on the line or
word (or these days even the syllable) where you start your
re-sing. Sometimes the engineer will put you in *input* mode
so that you can actually sing the lines up to the line you're
to re-sing although you're not actually recording the previous (roll time) lines again. That makes for a consistent vocal
on the fixed line. The engineer will "punch out" once you've
sung your re-sing line, but you need to keep singing so that
the breaths stay consistent with the previous vocal. *Run it
out*, just like a baseball player runs out the race for first base
even if the play is over. The engineer will probably check to
make sure the "punch" sounds natural—both the vocal part
and the edit.

I find that many times I want to re-sing the whole first verse
and chorus again after listening down. Many session singers
often begin to really lock into the groove on the second verse.
Singing the first part of the song again gives you a chance to
use the same confidence and energy that you've found in the
second verse and the rest of the song.

Other times, if you just can't seem to nail a tricky melody or phrasing, the producer will play the worktape for you
through your cans. This can give you a clearer idea of what the
writer intended. Sometimes the writer will be at the session;
if they're not there, refer to the worktape so that they don't
have to ask you to come back in for a re-sing at a later date.

Finally, let the producer decide when to move on. Never assume the vocal fix is perfect (even if it is). Remember, *you just work here.*

My hope is that you get on a roll with your session work. Once you do, you will likely be faced with a dilemma that many budding session singers face: You need the work but you're asked to sing material with which you do not want to be associated. After all, *you never know who will eventually hear the recording.*

What will you do?

CHAPTER 8

Prostitution Is Still Illegal in Most States, Isn't It?

Selecting Your Work Wisely Without Compromise

We've all done it. All of us who call ourselves professional session singers have at one time or another had to record songs for a client that were, shall we say, less than average. Studio pros grit their teeth and jokingly refer to this as "being a prostitute"—lowering their standards for a dollar. When work begins to come in, it's hard to turn anything down, but this can turn into a problem in the long run because session singers can often be associated with and identified by the quality of the material they record. This isn't so bad for session *players*, but the *singer* represents the song. We put our reputations on the line with every note we sing. As your voice becomes more recognizable and more work is offered, you will want to be careful with your selection of material to demo.

It's completely up to you what kind of songs you're willing to record. I do recommend that you give it some thought, though. You never know where your vocal work will wind up. Remember, perception is everything in the recording industry—or at least it looks that way!

The material you choose to record plays an integral part in establishing your own vocal style. Soon, you will be able to easily recognize songs for which you are best suited and songs that would better served by a different vocalist. In time, you'll *want* to turn down some songs, in order to develop your reputation. Clients call me if they've got a big soulful ballad or a pop crossover country song. They typically don't call me for traditional country songs, for rough rock songs, or for a lyric that is morally questionable. (That's something to consider as well when choosing material that you will or will not record, because you *will* be faced with this dilemma at some point.) Remember, reputations are built a session at a time.

Avoiding Stigmas

At the beginning of my career in Nashville I was asked to sing demos by songwriters at various levels of achievement in their own careers. It's often easier to convince newer writers, rather than the veterans, that you are worth their money. The problem is that many of them have only really unpolished songs to record. You think, "Nobody will ever hear these songs, anyway," so you agree to cut a vocal for them. Ah, but you can't be too careful. You never know what connections a new writer may have and who will hear you. It's possible that they'll get to know a music executive who will ask, "Who's the singer?" And then, just like that, you're associated with substandard material. Once again, it's *perception*. It's easy to be labeled a B-level session singer even when you've got the goods to be A-level.

In other words, sometimes no gig is better than a bad gig.

Older tunesmiths with a history in the industry can cause you inadvertently to be tagged with a different stigma. Don't get me wrong. I have great respect for the stalwarts of the business and have learned a great deal from them. Unfortunately, some shallow music execs believe that if you're not having current hits as a songwriter, then you must be old news. Sometimes those in a position to hire you for session work think that if you can manage only to work for the veterans of the field, then you must not have anything to offer the contemporary market. Suddenly you're perceived as out of fashion yourself, and it's a little harder to move into the contemporary circles. Still, I will always take an offer to work for the songwriting forefathers in our industry. There is plenty to learn from them.

By the way, the same stigma can apply in reverse. If you've been working with contemporary writers a lot, it can be harder to convince legendary writers or their publishers that you can render something more classic in nature.

I've been asked to do a lot of gospel music throughout my career, in part because my vocal work has been labeled soulful. In fact, I've recorded probably hundreds of songs for the gospel market. So when I was recommended to a late, great Country Music Hall of Fame songwriter, a living legend who has penned hundreds of legendary songs for everyone from Patsy Cline to George Jones, he was somewhat hesitant about using me to sing his songs, for fear that I would make them sound too "churchy" and not country enough.

But I knew that I had tons of experience singing country music and that I could do a fine job for him. I arrived at the studio knowing the material and dug into the song—a great, classic-sounding song that only this man could write. From behind the mic, I could see his white hair as he walked into the control room. He sat in a couch right in front of the window where I was singing his song. Remembering his apprehension to my singing his material, I was a bit nervous, though I never let it show. And after I'd done my best with the song, the engineer asked me to come in to the control room and listen. I walked in unsure of the legend's response. He stood up slowly and said, "Mak, you're one hell of a singer! I love it!"

Moments like these are one big reason why I still sing today. You'll find encouragement in your journey, too. But stay humble. Just stash the words of encouragement away and pull them out on a day when you really need them.

My advice to you to avoid being pigeonholed is to stay true to what you're naturally good at while continuing to grow and even bend slightly as a professional vocalist. You can stretch a little in your selection of work while still working to establish your own style. This takes time to develop, but many top session singers achieve reputations as unique yet versatile vocalists.

Here's something worth mentioning: You might lose a client for a while, simply because you've done too many of their demos and they or their publisher want to try a new voice to represent their songs. Don't be offended. Instead, earmark their name and number to call them in a few months while you pursue new business relationships.

Are you going to take *any* kind of session work for the money? I can't tell you the answer to that question. You'll have to decide for yourself. You do need to think before you act, though. You're building a business here.

Think of it this way: If you owned a restaurant, what clientele would you hope to serve? What clientele do you hope to serve in your studio work?

Got a Niche?

My little girl has some musical ability. Well-meaning friends have asked if my wife and I are going to have her take piano lessons. My response is, "I'd rather her learn the tuba or steel guitar. There are only a few working tuba-ists (?) and steel guitar players!" Of course, I'm only joking, yet there is truth in my response as it applies to the recording industry.

If you eventually earn recognition as the best at something specific, then you are more likely to get calls than a "general practitioner." I believe you can develop a niche and maintain more mainstream work, too. If there is one style of music where you really shine, the work will come to you. There is nothing wrong with developing a niche and doing other styles, too, as long as you're being true to your natural style. You might even develop a strength within your style that will garner some attention from record execs, if that's your goal. At the very least, you will get calls from writers whose writing strength is your vocal strength, and together you'll make a great recording!

One of my favorite clients is another Hall of Fame composer, who wrote enormous hits in the 1970s and '80s, when melodic pop/ country with moving lyrics sold millions of albums. Wisely, he is selective about casting session singers to work on his material. If I'm not right for his latest creation, he won't call me—and rightfully so. When he does, he calls and says something like "Mak, I've got one that I think you'd be perfect for. Can you come sing it?" He has never failed to cast perfectly. I have never felt the least bit out of my element recording for him. The songs that he has me sing are perfect fits for my vocal style. I've often told him that I would love to record a whole album's worth of his material someday.

One key to being a hit songwriter is knowing how to cast the session singers that fit the songs stylistically. When you find that songwriter/session singer fit, it's a beautiful thing. That's something to strive for as you pursue success. As a matter of fact, that is success!

Still, you want to avoid being pigeonholed if you have strengths in other areas too. Don't get stuck in your niche. Even if the same writer/producers call you for a particular vocal style, you can still pursue others as you market your versatility. If establishing a career as a versatile vocalist is your goal, collect copies of your sessions that represent a variety of styles and market yourself in that manner.

But how do you find the type of material that you want to record? Go straight to the source!

How to Record the Material You Want to Record

If there are songwriters whose work you particularly like, read the liner notes in the CDs where their songs appear, find the names of their music publishers, and do a Google or some other online search for the listed publishers. You can also search the sites of the major performing rights organizations (BMI, ASCAP, SESAC) to find the writers and their publisher(s). Then you may call a particular publisher and ask if you can deliver or send them a demo CD. You may or may not be able to do work for your very favorite songwriter, but at least you can pursue work with a publisher whose taste in writers is similar to yours.

I've had the opportunity to sing demos for many of my musical heroes. A couple of them were signed to one particular music-publishing company with headquarters in Nashville. I got to know the creative director quite well as I pursued work at the company. It was through our friendship that I was asked to sing demos for these writers whose work I love so much.

By building good relationships with music publishers whose stables include writers that you respect, you may earn the opportunity to actually work with those writers. You could become a critical part of the puzzle that helps those writers get their songs on the radio. Sometimes that process begins by building good business relationships with the music publishers.

But you can also go directly to the songwriters. Music cities such as Nashville often have writers clubs with writers' nights. I've played most of them, and I've also met lots of great songwriters in the venues simply by going to their shows and introducing myself to them after the show. That is a great way to acquire the work you really want.

If you hear a songwriter at one of these writers' shows whose material knocks you out, give them your demo CD and ask them to keep you in mind for any of their song demos. Let them know you're a fan. Remember, songwriters want to know that you're passionate about their material. Don't fabricate this! Approach only the writers whose songs you want to record. Be diplomatic: Don't offend the ones who sing by telling them that your vocals will improve their song pitches. Instead, tell them that while their singing is really good, they could call you if they ever want to try a different vocal. I've done plenty of vocals for phenomenal singer/songwriters who just want to try a fresh approach.

Artists can be intimidated by demos sung by former session newcomers who have since turned into superstars, so a new session vocalist is sometimes needed for an old demo. Certain demos that were recorded a while back might also be considered "dated material," in which case a songwriter or music publisher will have a new demo cut, with a new session singer, so that song can make the rounds once again.

To sum up, strive for integrity in your work. That begins by staying true to who you are vocally and recording the songs that you care about. Locate the music publishers and songwriters whose material you want to record and you'll sleep better at night, knowing that you're recording songs that suit your taste and style.

CHAPTER 9

Fixing the Books

Run Your Session Business Smoothly

To make session singing your business, treat it like one. This requires good bookkeeping. As your work picks up, find a good accountant who specializes in the entertainment industry. The accountant's responsibilities can range from handling your taxes quarterly or annually to keeping you fiscally organized. A good bookkeeper, experienced in the music industry, can also meet this task. Ask your colleagues for names and numbers of professionals whom they trust. Interview them.

Until your business gets to a point where you're working too much to keep up with your paperwork yourself, there are good and simple habits to develop to keep your business organized.

Keep a paper trail and/or computer file of

(1) your session dates, including names and locations of the studios and names of the producers;

(2) how much you were either paid or are owed for the session;

(3) all bank deposit receipts; and

(4) all expense receipts, kept in separate envelopes.

This is all the information that an accountant will need to prepare your taxes. Remember, organization = control. Looking at your income and expenses in black and white gives you incentive to hustle up business and to keep your expenditures to a minimum.

If you keep these records on your computer, back up all of your files. Speak with an accountant or a computer store about which software programs can assist you with various bookkeeping chores. Keeping good books will aid you in tax preparation and give you control over your business.

Now, let's break your records down into the components that will give you control over your business.

1. Session Dates

Keep track of your calendar with a hard-copy organizer or an electronic organizer located in your computer, cell phone, or other device. Make sure that you back up any electronic data. I recommend keeping a hard-copy file *and* an electronic file. As soon as you receive a call for a session, ask the client if you can put that in the books as a confirmed date. If it's tentative, write it in pencil.

Hopefully, your schedule will pick up to the point that you're occasionally *double-booked*—that is, you've been called to do more than one session in the same time slot. That's a good problem. When that occurs, you will need to ask if one of the clients can move their session time. If they really want you, they will move it. If they can't, at least you already have the time booked. Let the client know that you're sorry you couldn't make this session and that you hope they will call you for the next one. Being in demand keeps clients interested. They know you're good if you're working a lot.

By the way, to avoid confusion in your bookkeeping, your fee should always remain the same, regardless of the client, though it should also gradually increase with time and experience. We will talk about fees in just a moment.

Write down or enter in your session date, the time of the session (I always write down 15 minutes earlier than the actual session time so that I'm definitely prompt if not early), the name and location of the studio (with directions if needed), and the client's name and contact information. Always ask for a cell phone number in case you get lost and need to call for directions. Smaller studios don't usually answer the phone when a session is in progress, and larger studios can be too busy to relay a message, so be prepared and have the client's cell phone number handy.

If there is any specific information about the session that you need to add to your notes, do it. Knowledge is power. The more information you have going into a session, the better it will go.

2. How Much You Were Paid or Owed

Keep a file for every session you do and account for the amount you were paid. This file can also help you keep track of companies and individuals that owe you for a session. Also, your checks can be photocopied and kept in a folder. In case you forget, you will still want to note in your file what you were paid for each session.

It's a known fact in professional recording circles that with the major conglomerate companies it can take up to 60 days before you receive your amount due. Independent publishers and songwriters typically pay a lot quicker; many times you'll get your fee on the spot. A check from an independent will not have taxes deducted, so you will need to know your state's tax percentage and deduct it yourself. I highly recommend that you stash the tax money in an interest bearing account and draw from it quarterly to pay your taxes. An accountant will help you to establish a payment schedule with the IRS.

You'll need a template for a professional invoice. Many clients require that you email or snail-mail an invoice for their expense records. Most document programs in your computer will have good invoice templates. Of course, you can also have your own design printed. Your invoice should state the date of the session, To: [your client's name and contact information], From: [your name and contact information], the songs you worked on, your fee, and your billing address. The easier it is to read, the better.

3. Bank Deposit Receipts

Audits are commonplace within the music industry. My advice is to keep every documented proof of transaction for added protection from an audit. This includes bank deposits. The envelope or folder system is always best. It's a good idea to keep your check deposit receipts with your checks.

4. Expense Receipts

Try your best to break even with the IRS. (Good luck!) Your accountant can inform you of legitimate tax deductions; keep receipts to prove these deductions. For instance, if you go out to eat between sessions, keep your restaurant receipts. There are automobile and gasoline deductions. There are deductions you can take for gear, such as headphones and even office supplies. Your first couple of years could be a business loss if your expenses are greater than your income. That's okay because you will most likely get a tax refund those years. Again, ask your accountant about the deductions you can take.

A couple of years ago I got a call from my wife, who takes care of some of my paperwork. A notice had arrived from the IRS, rubber-stamped in red ink that screamed "Urgent!" That'll rattle your *nerves. I asked her to open it right away. "Oh, my gosh, honey," she said. "They say you owe taxes on $83,000 that you didn't report!"*

Fortunately, we had saved the W-9 that this client had sent me. It turns out that someone at the IRS couldn't read decimals! I had done only $830.00 worth of work for this client that previous year. Thankfully, that client sent a letter to the IRS for us and straightened the whole thing out.

There are two morals to this story. First of all, I had built a good enough business relationship with the client that he went out of his way to help us clear this IRS blunder up. Secondly, we were reminded of just how important it is to keep good records.

Taxes

Again, it's a good decision to employ the services of an accountant once your business begins to build. Your accountant can set up a tax-payment plan for you and assist in building your business by advising you about ways to save money on taxes. Keep up with your payments and you won't get in the hole.

Be "above-board." Under-the-table cash transactions can come back to bite you. It can be a temptation to pull one over on the IRS by accepting cash payment without reporting it, but integrity means doing the right thing even when the IRS isn't watching!

The Union

As a session vocalist, you will need to know about AFTRA (American Federation of Television and Recording Artists), the union for professional vocalists. With any union affiliation there are pros and cons. I am neither endorsing nor opposing the union. Affiliating with the union is entirely your decision.

Many of the major studios are union *signatories* and require that only union-member vocalists work in them. Many studios are not union signatories and don't care if you're a non–union member. In any event, it is rare that you will lose out on work because you're not a member.

There are benefits to being an AFTRA member. You are guaranteed a minimum rate for each session. You are also entitled access to insurance, retirement benefits, and scholarships through the union. When you are featured on widely distributed recordings or soundtracks, the union can help you negotiate and collect payment for your sessions. Professional performers who wish to join AFTRA should contact their local AFTRA office or the national membership department to find out about the services it provides and how to join. AFTRA's Web site has quite a bit of information, including a list of session vocalists in your town who are AFTRA members.

New members must complete an application and pay a one-time initiation fee and dues for the current dues period. The initiation fee is currently $1,300 and, as of January 2007, minimum dues are $63.90 every six months.

For union sessions, the studio manager or owner and the union session singer must sign an agreement prior to the session. This will guarantee your rate, including the insurance premium or other added benefits. It also keeps the studio owner in good standing with the union. If you aren't singing *on the card* (that is, you aren't a union session singer and therefore haven't filled out the proper union paperwork) and the client is a signatory, then you may actually be paid through the union although you're not a member. If that happens enough, a union representative may ask you to join AFTRA at that point. You still have the right to decline or to accept.

Rates

Union scale for demo work is set by AFTRA, and a minimum must be met by the client. Check with your local AFTRA office for rates.

New session demo singers who aren't affiliated with the union can expect to start as low as $40–$50 per song. You may even want to offer a lower fee just to get in the door with some clients and then raise your fee after establishing a steady working relationship, maybe up to $75 per song, for instance. After building your reputation over several more years, you can ask a minimum fee of $100 or even $125 per song. (As I stated earlier, my personal rate is based on per hour or per song, whichever comes first.)

A demo shouldn't take an hour to record for a professional vocalist. If you are asked to sing more than three songs, the rate can be lowered slightly per song.

Here is important information for writers, music publishers, and producers: The more songs you can have on your session, the better the rate. You're going to pay less per song if you're doing a four-song session as opposed to a two-song session. Since studio time slots are often from ten in the morning until two in the afternoon, and from two o'clock until six o'clock, you will find that four songs is a good number to record per session, with instrumental tracking in the morning session and vocals in the afternoon.

Tips for the Self-Employed Session Singer

Small business is big business. Find out as much as you can about running your own small business. Take continuing education courses if you can afford it, pick up books at the library on the subject of building your small business, and research small-business tips on the Internet. Know as much as you can about maximizing your business as a studio professional. There are organizations that can assist you as a small-business person. Stay informed so that you can conduct your business on the level and in an up-to-date fashion. The resources I just mentioned will help you find tips for success, ways to save money, and ways to make money.

Being a session singer is serious business—treat it that way. Build your business and your reputation one session at a time!

By conducting your business in a professional manner, you will attract more and better clients. In fact, if you handle your business like a pro, you could soon be the talk of the town.

CHAPTER 10

Hot Gossip

Becoming the Talk of the Town

You want your reputation to precede you. It's a great feeling when someone you meet for the first time at an industry
function already knows your work or at least your name. Let's
assume this is starting to happen more frequently. You're on
a roll. Calls are coming in for sessions. Your datebook is full.
(Yes, it can happen!)

What Now?

It seems as if the work will never slow down—oh, but it will, if
you don't do a couple of very important things to keep the mo-
mentum going. You need to make time to stay in touch with clients. Do this on your cell phone between sessions. You can also
drop in on them from time to time. The beauty of the recording
industry in Nashville is that many of the recording studios are
in close proximity to one another; you can even walk from one
to another along Music Row or in the Berry Hill neighborhood.
Music publishers and commercial jingle companies are sprinkled
throughout the town as well. Your clients are never too far away
to contact and to see what projects they're currently working on.

Here are the two things you can do to keep the ball rolling:

(1) stay in touch with your clients either by phone or email or in person on a regular basis (remembering that relationships are a major secret to success); and:

(2) send thank-you notes to your longstanding clients via email, or follow up with a call just to say "thanks" to new clients (no kidding!).

1. Stay in Touch

One of the best session singers, someone with a long career in Nashville, once told me that he took one day out of every month just to call his clients. Staying in touch will let them know that you care about their work. You'll be building good business relationships this way. You might begin a conversation with a client by asking if they have received any feedback on the last session you guys worked on together. The response will likely have been positive. If so, there's your chance to say something like, "Well, I hope we can do it again real soon!" If the response to the client's session was negative, you can say something like, "Is there something I can do differently next time?" Let your client know that you'll do your best to help them succeed. Do your best to stay on their radar screens by staying in touch with them. They just might be finishing up a song that they would like for you to sing for them. Good timing is part of success in the music industry, so your chances for success increase the more you're in touch with your clients.

2. "Thank Ya Very Much"

The courtesy of a thank-you note has fallen by the wayside in this age of technology. That's a shame. Clients find it refreshing when they receive a note of appreciation. I encourage you to go that extra mile and follow up with a thank-you note after your session. It's another way of staying in touch with your clients and, therefore, staying on their minds. It also shows professional courtesy, which everyone appreciates.

If you have their email address, shoot them an email. If not, a quick message on their voicemail will be just as nice. You might say something like "I just want to thank you for choosing me to sing your songs. It was a real pleasure. I hope you'll keep me in mind for your next batch of hits!"

My last staff writer position with a music publisher had dissolved as they often do in this industry, and I decided to pursue opportunities to teach and counsel young people who hoped to enter the recording industry. I wanted a position that would let me give back to the business while continuing to write songs and do session work. After pulling together my résumé, I met with the audio engineering school faculty where I now have my Music Row office. We discussed my recording industry experience and their expectations of me.

I went home and immediately composed an email to thank them for their time and consideration. I reiterated specific subjects we had discussed and even mentioned a couple of things we had not discussed. Most of all, I let them know that I appreciated the opportunity to meet with them.

The next day, I received a phone call asking me to join their staff. I later found out that they had needed to make a decision between another candidate and me. They told me that the clincher was the thank-you note they received from me just after the interview. Apparently, I had the courtesy, follow-up, and communication skills they needed for that position.

A genuine "thank you" isn't heard often enough today, yet it goes a long way in this very personal business.

A Summary of Secrets

Let's review some of the secrets of success that I've shared with you. Refer to them often to stay fresh in your pursuit of success as a session singer. Even after you find yourself working behind the mic often, you will sometimes need a fresh approach. It's never too early or too late to develop good business habits that will benefit your career.

Remember your "Six Safecrackers" as you attempt to crack open the airtight doors of the recording industry: Talent, Confidence, Courtesy—Tenacity, Courage, and Commitment (TCC—TCC)!

Build good business relationships. This is the best way to have a long, smooth ride in a career that can sometimes feel more like a roller coaster ride.

Stay on top of your game vocally by taking care of your voice and using it regularly.

Keep your chin up in the down time! Use "down time" to your advantage. Hone your skills and strengthen your voice. Practice, practice, practice.

Be prepared! Always remember this: Time is money in the studio and your client wants to save money. Therefore, you can't be *too* prepared. Do your homework and know the material when you step behind the mic.

Establish good communication with the guys in the control room. The engineer is your greatest ally.

Size matters. The smaller your ego, the better. In fact, leave your ego outside the door.

Remember, it's about the song! Ask yourself, "What can I do to make the song better?" and not "How can I best be heard?"

Build a reputation of integrity and maintain an attitude of excellence. It will pay off!

Behind the mic, remember that it's less about singing than it is about communicating well. A vocal session is less about *performance* than it is about having a *sincere conversation* through song with your listener.

Learn to listen well. Listen to your work from various vantage points.

Select your work wisely, without compromise! What clientele would you like to serve?

Continue to grow, but find your niche. Be the "go-to guy [or girl]" for a certain style, but stretch when possible.

Organization = control. Keep good records. Treat your career as a serious business.

Stay in touch with your clients. Let your clients know that you care about their work and their success. And finally . . .

Build your business and your reputation one session at a time!

I am humbled every time one of the most successful composers in the music industry calls *me* for a session. Some of their quotes grace the promotional material that accompanies this project. I am truly humbled because these writers are some of my heroes. No, I'm not among the richest and most famous people in Nashville, but I am blessed to work with some of the best songwriters and producers this industry has to offer. It didn't happen overnight. I've been singing professionally for 27 years and receiving payment for studio work for nearly 25 of those years. Each session is an opportunity to build my reputation as well as my business.

I've talked a lot about the importance of building good business relationships because that is the absolute most important thing you can do to be successful. The relationships that you build lead to other relationships, to greater opportunities to be your best, and to other modes of income. You will have opportunities to grow as a person, as a vocalist, and as a professional as you build your own business relationships.

If you take these secrets of success "behind the mic" with you in your pursuit of recording excellence, you will no doubt

have your own wonderful session confessions to share someday.

Thank you for reading some of mine.

All the best!

CD Credits

All music herein is a product of MKM Productions.
"In the Meantime" written by Mak Kaylor
Copyright © by Mak Kaylor Music (SESAC) 2006, a division
    of MKM Productions

Vocalist: Mak Kaylor (www.makkaylor.com)
Keyboards: Don Bradley
Voiceover: Don Scott Hare for Don Scott Hare Productions
Engineer: John Albani

Recorded at Sonic Eden Studios (www.sonicedenstudios.com)